*Also by Geraldine McCaughrean*

*Britannia:* 100 *Great Stories from British History*
illustrated by Richard Brassey
*Stories from Shakespeare*
*God's People*
*God's Kingdom*
*Golden Myths and Legends*
*Silver Myths and Legends*

# BRITANNIA
## *on Stage*

### 25 Plays from
### British History

Geraldine McCaughrean
Illustrated by Richard Brassey

Dolphin Paperbacks

First published in 2000
as a Dolphin paperback
by Orion Children's Books
a division of the Orion Publishing Group Ltd
Orion House
5 Upper Saint Martin's Lane
London WC2H 9EA

A catalogue record for this book is
available from the British Library.

Typeset at The Spartan Press Ltd,
Lymington, Hants

Printed in Great Britain
by The Guernsey Press Co. Ltd, Guernsey, C. I.

ISBN 1 85881 799 4

# CONTENTS

I am indebted to the drama students and staff at St Gabriel's School, Newbury for their invaluable help in shaping the written word into living theatre. This book is for them.

# INTRODUCTION

Here are twenty-five one-act playlets re-enacting colourful, legendary moments in the history of our nation – not factual in every case, perhaps, but moments which so caught the imagination that they were retold time after time, and so migrated into folklore. While historians wrestled with detail and proof, this was what ordinary people considered history: a hugger-mugger treasury of adventure, comedy, tragedy, heroes and villains.

You are unlikely to want to stage every one of the twenty-five. You may well want to pick and choose a dozen in order to assemble an enjoyable hour or two for your audience. But we have provided a wide enough selection for you to suit your choice to a particular term's curriculum, to the performers available, to incorporate stories of local interest or simply stage your favourites.

Alternatively, they could be performed one per week during the year – during class assemblies, perhaps.

Playlets requiring large casts have been interspersed with others requiring only a handful of actors; in the latter, you may wish to cast extrovert, talented children or drama club members. Not only do small scenes add dramatic variety, they also allow time backstage to marshal actors for the next large-scale play.

Attached to each is a list of characters. Listed, too, are any costumes, props and special effects recommended, although experience has shown me that these need to be kept to the absolute minimum – ideally, just one item per character. Audiences are unlikely to quibble at anachronistic touches such as electric torches or sunglasses and hair gel, if these make for easy scene-setting or good dramatic effect.

The stage directions included imply that the plays will

be performed on a proscenium stage, but this is by no means necessary. During development, ten of these plays were performed in the round, by a single band of female actors dressed in black and armed with a simple 'property basket' of costume and props. (There is a lot to be said for simplicity.) The actors entered in the role of 'Jolly Jack and his company of players', which effectively explained away the lack of elaborate sets, props and costumes, and served to unify a motley assortment of stories. It worked extremely well, and for that reason we have included these 'entrances and exits' at the end of the book under the title of 'Jolly Jack', in case you would like to use them too.

A programme note has been added to each play, to provide a 'self-assembly' programme which puts an audience in the picture as to date, setting and background of each scene.

These plays arose out of a much bigger work: *Britannia: 100 Great Stories from British History.* Naturally, the easiest way into performing any of them is for children to read (or be read) the story in its original form before tackling the play script.

Geraldine McCaughrean

# The Tin Islands
## about 100BC

*Programme note*

Two thousand years ago, British mines were the sole source of tin in a Europe clamouring for bronze tools and weapons.

The Phoenicians, intrepid international merchants, carried British tin to the Mediterranean, and sold it to the Romans. Naturally, the Romans were anxious to find and conquer these 'Islands of Tin' for themselves. The Phoenicians were equally anxious they should not.

## Cast

PHOENICIAN CAPTAIN
6 PHOENICIAN CREW
ROMAN CAPTAIN
6 ROMAN CREW
CYMBAL-PLAYER, off stage

## Costumes

- Roman helmets
- Phoenician caps or plain, knitted hats

## Props

- 2 ships' wheels (cardboard cut-outs)
- 2 lengths of rope, say 4 metres long
- large sheet of tin, e.g. a baking tray
- cymbals, off stage
- a large 'rock'

## Special Effects

- optional recording of seagulls and sea

## Idea!

A 'Mexican Wave' would be very effective, though younger children might find it difficult to combine words and motions.

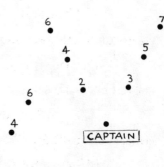

# THE TIN ISLANDS

*The crews of two 'ships', one* PHOENICIAN, *one* ROMAN, *are on stage. Frontmost in each is the* CAPTAIN, *holding a ship's wheel, and behind him stand his* CREW, *arrayed as shown. A rope 'contains' each group, representing the ship's rail. The* CREW MEMBERS *hold on to this rope and sway in unison. There is a large rock centre stage front.* PHOENICIAN 2 *is holding a large tin tray.*

ROMAN CAPTAIN: (pointing at the Phoenician ship) Now I have you, you water gypsy! Put on more sail, men, and follow that ship!

PHOENICIAN CAPTAIN: So! You are after my secret, are you, Roman? You, with your crew of fairweather sailors? In a ship built for summer seas? You won't like where I lead you, but catch me if you can! Turning east!

PHOENICIAN 1: East!

    (*All* PHOENICIAN CREW *turn to face left*)

ROMAN CAPTAIN: East!

    (*All* ROMAN CREW *turn to face left*)

PHOENICIAN CAPTAIN: South!

    (*All* PHOENICIANS *turn to face upstage . . .*)

ROMAN CAPTAIN: South!

    (*. . . All the* ROMANS *do the same*)

PHOENICIAN CAPTAIN: West!

    (*All* PHOENICIANS *turn to face left . . .*)

ROMAN CAPTAIN: West!

(*. . . All the* ROMANS *do the same*)

PHOENICIAN CAPTAIN: North!

(*All the* PHOENICIANS *turn to face the front . . .*)

ROMAN CAPTAIN: North!

(*. . . All the* ROMANS *do the same*)

ROMAN 1: Where are you taking us, Captain?

ROMAN CAPTAIN: To the Tin Islands! To the land where the tin comes from!

PHOENICIAN 2: This is what he is after.

(*Produces tin sheet and rattles it*)

ALL: Tin!!

PHOENICIAN CAPTAIN: The most valuable commodity to a nation of soldiers, and only I know where it can be had.

PHOENICIAN 3: We Phoenicians trade dye and pottery, cloth and furs with the people of the Tin Islands . . .

PHOENICIAN 4: . . . wild, woolly, woad-painted people.

PHOENICIAN 5: . . . and sell it to the people of the Mediterranean.

PHOENICIAN 6: The Romans are our best customers.

PHOENICIAN 1: Naturally, they'd like to cut us out – find the Tin Islands themselves, and add them to their Roman Empire.

PHOENICIAN CAPTAIN: But I shan't be the one to betray our secret. Not if I can help it. Turning east!

PHOENICIAN 1: East!

(PHOENICIAN CREW *turn to face left*)

ROMAN CAPTAIN: East!

(ROMAN CREW *turn to face left*)

PHOENICIAN CAPTAIN: South!

(*As before*)

ROMAN CAPTAIN: South!

PHOENICIAN CAPTAIN: West!

ROMAN CAPTAIN: West!

PHOENICIAN CAPTAIN: North!

ROMAN CAPTAIN: North!

ROMAN 1: Where are you taking us, Captain?

ROMAN 2: We never sailed in waters so grey.

ROMAN 3: We never sailed in waters so rough.

ROMAN 4: We never sailed in waters so cold.

ROMAN 5: We never felt so scared!

ROMAN 6: We never felt so sick!

(*They are all sick over the side*)

ROMAN CAPTAIN: But think of the wealth awaiting the man who finds the legendary Tin Islands! Think of the glory!

ALL: Land ho!

PHOENICIAN 6: He's still following, Captain.

PHOENICIAN 4: He sticks to us like a barnacle.

PHOENICIAN CAPTAIN: Then like a barnacle we must scrape him off!

(*He steers sharply and the* CREW *all reel sideways*)

PHOENICIAN 3: The mists are thick.

PHOENICIAN 2: The surf is rough.

PHOENICIAN 1: Must we sail so close to the shore?

PHOENICIAN CAPTAIN: I know these waters and he doesn't. He'll run aground on the rocks.

ROMAN CAPTAIN: He knows these waters. Follow in his wake and he'll guide us through the rocks.

PHOENICIAN 6: He's still following, Captain.

PHOENICIAN 3 AND ROMAN 3: The mists are thick.

PHOENICIAN 2 AND ROMAN 2: The sea is rough.

PHOENICIAN 1 AND ROMAN 1: The weather is getting worse.

(*Rattle of tin tray to represent thunder*)

PHOENICIAN 4 AND ROMAN 4: What secret is worth this kind of risk?

ALL: Tin!!

PHOENICIAN CAPTAIN: (shakes fist at pursuing Romans) Since I can't throw you off, I shall lead you where you never thought to go. They mustn't find out our secret. The wealth of our whole people depends on it. I'm running her aground, men! When she strikes, swim for the shore!

(*Rattle of tin tray, plus clash of cymbals off. All* PHOENI-CIANS *fall to their knees and start 'swimming' and 'drowning'. The two* CAPTAINS *roll behind the rock centre stage. Another cymbal clash off stage*)

ROMANS: (variously) We're aground! Abandon ship! Swim for the shore! We're sinking!

(*Ominous trembling of tin tray*)

PHOENICIAN CAPTAIN: (*pulls himself out on to the rock, from behind it, so as to appear over the top, gasping*) The secret is safe now. Safe with the sea.

ROMAN CAPTAIN: (*pulling himself out on to the same rock from behind*) For a while, maybe. But one day. One day . . .

# The Resting Place
about AD50

## *Programme note*

Legend has it that Christ himself visited England as a boy, along with his uncle, Joseph of Arimathea. After the crucifixion, Joseph is reputed to have returned to England's Somerset, carrying the Holy Grail. This is the story of how he chose the site for his community of disciples.

## Cast

JESUS CHRIST

JOSEPH OF ARIMATHEA

5 (OR MORE) CHORUS

ANGEL

## Costumes

- Jesus could be dressed in contemporary clothes and wrap-round robe
- monks' habits
- various tunics and tunic dresses

## Props

- scattering of rocks
- bucket of soil hidden by 'grass'
- long walking-staff with a hole in the top
- spray of artificial white blossom
- cheap wooden goblet
- map – antique scroll or Ordnance Survey, as preferred

## Special Effects

- optional recorded birdsong

## Idea!

Have the cast discuss whether or not they believe Christ may have come here, and look at Joseph of Arimathea's role in the story of the Passion. What do they know about the Holy Grail and the later myths that surround it? What other legends are there of the Holy Family visiting England?

# THE RESTING PLACE

*The scene is a hilltop. A few rocks are scattered around and there is a bucket of earth concealed by a cardboard flat, painted to represent a grassy tussock*

*(The chorus sit along the front of the stage. They chant mechanically, as in 'what's the time, Mr Wolf')*

CHORUS: What's the time, mister?

JESUS CHRIST: In China, Ran Mang of the Han Dynasty is Emperor.

CHORUS: What's the time, mister?

JESUS CHRIST: Tiberius Caesar has just come to power. The philosopher Seneca is teaching a young Nero his letters.

CHORUS: What's the time, mister?

JESUS CHRIST: In Japan, wrestling has just been invented; in Europe the oboe.

CHORUS: What's the time, mister?

JESUS CHRIST: Time for Rome to conquer this country, just as it conquered mine.

CHORUS: What's the time, mister?

JESUS CHRIST: Half past dawn and quarter to twilight.

CHORUS: What's the time, mister?

JESUS CHRIST: What does it matter? Up here? On top of a hill, time ceases to travel in a straight line. It circles. Day and night circle like birds – white pigeons, black crows. The countryside below turns green and yellow, ripens into gold and berry red, freezes into this spiteful white. There's magic at the top of a hill. It could be the first day of Time or the last.

CHORUS: Time to go, mister.

JESUS CHRIST: Yes. Yes. Time to go down. Time to set the clocks ticking again. Time to restart the calendars. Time to go back to the country where I grew up . . . But I'd rather stay here, I don't mind telling you. Up here on the top of this English hill circled with rings of bright frozen water. I'm afraid. Think of me, won't you, the next time you stand here? The next time you stand on an English hilltop, with the birds circling overhead.

(JESUS CHRIST *pulls on a 'Jesus-type' coat-robe and all exit. The* CHORUS *get up and become the* FOLLOWERS *of* JOSEPH. *They are worn out, starting to whinge, trudging up to the top of the same hill, with* JOSEPH *leading the way*)

FOLLOWER 1: How much further, master?

FOLLOWER 2: We've been travelling without stop for weeks – months!

FOLLOWER 3: This country is all mud and thistles and ice.

JOSEPH: I can see Glass Island! Come on, brothers. Just a little further!

(FOLLOWERS *all sit down, worn out*)

All right, then. Rest a bit. We're all weary. We've come a long way.

FOLLOWER 1: First the sea voyage out of Tyre.

FOLLOWER 2: Across the Mediterranean.

FOLLOWER 3: Past the Pillars of Hercules.

FOLLOWER 4: Round Finis Terre – the end of the world.

FOLLOWER 5: Into that choppy, grey ocean.

FOLLOWER 1: Up that great muddy estuary.

FOLLOWER 2: And across the frozen marshes of the Summer Land.

FOLLOWER 3: How can anyone call this the Summer Land?

FOLLOWER 4: (*consulting a map*) Here's Glass Island. So we must be here. This hill doesn't even have a name.

FOLLOWER 5: I could call it a few names. All-Worn-Out-Hill, that's what I'd call it.

JOSEPH: That's Glass Island – just over there. Do you see?

ALL FOLLOWERS: But we're worn out!

JOSEPH: (*grudgingly*) Very well. Rest yourselves. Sleep. Tomorrow we'll get there.

(*They all curl up, wrapped in their cloaks, but* JOSEPH *sits thinking*)

(*To audience*) There's something magic about the crest of a hill. Even the pagans sense it. Cut off from the workaday world down below. Up among the birds. Close to the sky.

(*Looks round, startled by knowing the place*)

I came here once with my nephew when he was a boy! No. What am I saying? Couldn't have been here, exactly. But somewhere like it. He loved the hills, loved to roam about singing at the top of his voice . . . That was before he began his work; before he set out to change the world. Before they killed him.

(*Takes out a wooden chalice and studies it fondly*)

That happened on a hilltop, too. Outside Jerusalem.

(*Angrily he jumps up*)

They made him carry his own gallows tree through the

streets, out into the countryside. It was baking hot – not like here. (*Shivers*) They set it up at the top of a hill.

(*He drives his staff into the bucket of earth, to demonstrate*)

A crude wooden cross and two more, one on either side. They nailed him to it and let him die of thirst and suffocation and pain. And for what? He'd done nothing. It's just that he shone too bright in their eyes: they had to snuff him out. People feel safer deep down in the dark.

(*He curls up to sleep again. Enter an* ANGEL, *holding a spray of white blossom which he shakes over the sleeping* JOSEPH)

ANGEL: Rest here, Joseph of Arimathea. Build here. Where is the cup you lent to your nephew at Passover? Where is the cup he drank from at his last supper?

(JOSEPH *stirs in his sleep; the cup rolls out of his hand.* ANGEL *picks it up*)

In years to come, kings and knights will account this the greatest treasure in all the world, and spend their lives in search of it. I shall hide it where only the purest and best will think to look.

(*He slots the blossom into the top of the staff before leaving. Birdsong begins. After a time, the* FOLLOWERS *start to wake up and stretch themselves*)

FOLLOWER 1: Wherever are we? I forget.

FOLLOWER 2: On top of a hill in f-f-freezing Summer Land.

FOLLOWER 3: What day is it? I lose track.

FOLLOWER 4: (*springing awake*) It's the Feast of the Nativity, that's what! It's Christmas Day!

(*His announcement changes everyone's mood*)

JOSEPH: (*jumps up and ranges round the stage*) And I had such a dream last night! This is the place, men! This is where we are meant to build our church.

FOLLOWER 5: (*unfolds the map*) But I thought . . .

JOSEPH: I know! I know! So did I! But an angel spoke to me last night, and told me to build right here – on Weary-All Hill!

FOLLOWER 1: (*picking up two rocks*) Shall we build in stone?

FOLLOWER 2: (*inspired*) No! A stable was good enough for him when he came into the world! Wattle and daub for us!

FOLLOWER 3: But shouldn't it be beautiful? A temple to the Lord?

JOSEPH: What could be more beautiful than this view? The English countryside! And listen! The birds are already singing carols!

FOLLOWER 4: Birdsong? In the middle of winter?

FOLLOWER 1: Let's start building!

FOLLOWER 2: I'm not tired any more.

FOLLOWER 3: I'm not cold any more.

FOLLOWER 4: I'm not even homesick any more.

FOLLOWER 5: (*exultant*) We shall look out from the top of Weary-All Hill for the rest of our lives, and be buried here when we die!

(*Their eyes converge on the staff*)

Master Joseph! Look at your staff!

FOLLOWER 1: It's taken root!

FOLLOWER 2: It's in blossom!

FOLLOWER 3: In the depths of winter.

FOLLOWER 4: It's a miracle!

FOLLOWER 5: A Christmas miracle.

JOSEPH: What else would you expect? It was the same with him. They buried him in the tomb – in my tomb – thinking they were rid of him. But he rose up again, like spring breaking free of winter. He rose up! High as a lark over a hill. Didn't I say there was magic at the top of hills? Let's find wood and start building!

# The Hallelujah Victory

## 429

## *Programme note*

Bishop Germanus was visiting Britain when it was invaded by a combined army of invading Picts, Scots and Saxons. The Roman legions had withdrawn back to Italy; the Britons were hugely outnumbered and hopelessly unprepared. But Germanus suggested a way in which the landscape itself might fight on behalf of the Britons . . .

## Cast

GERMANUS, a tall, imposing person

AT LEAST 8 BRITONS (dark-haired for preference),
including one very small person and one planted in
the audience

AT LEAST 10 SAXONS/PICTS/SCOTS (blond and red-
haired for preference)

## Costumes

- monk's habit
- nondescript tunics
- sandals for some

## Props

- bishop's crook and mitre
- clubs, spears, knives, swords for the invaders to carry
- several hand-sized mirrors (if relevant)
- large prompt card reading HALLELUJAH

## Special Effects

- flashing heliograms around the hall will only work
with a high, bright source of light
- I envisage the Britons climbing wall bars around the
room, in readiness for the ambush, but you may think
this too dangerous: e.g. they must not climb while holding a mirror in one hand

## Idea!

This play is ideal where the study of sound waves or
reflection of light are on the curriculum.

# THE HALLELUJAH VICTORY

*The staging here assumes a central aisle through the auditorium, with the* INVADERS *entering from the rear of the hall and moving towards the stage. One actor is seated anonymously in the audience. There is a blackboard and easel at the rear centre of the stage.* GERMANUS *stands stage right.*

(*The* BRITONS *rush on from stage left*)

ALL BRITONS: They're coming!

BRITON 1: They're coming! The Picts!

BRITON 2: They're coming! The Scots!

BRITON 3: They're coming! The Saxons!

BRITON 4: (*falls to his knees at* GERMANUS'S *feet*) You have to help us, Your Reverence!

GERMANUS: Peace, child. Calm yourself.

BRITON 1: The Romans have deserted us!

BRITON 2: The legions have left us all alone.

BRITON 3: We sent to Rome for help, but they ignored us.

BRITON 4: You have to help us, Your Holiness!

GERMANUS: The Romans were invaders here once. And yet you miss them now like sheep missing their shepherds.

BRITON 1: At least they knew how to fight the Picts.

BRITON 2: And we'll go like lambs to the slaughter if you don't help us.

GERMANUS: Me? A man of the cloth? A bishop of the

Church? What do I know about war? What do you expect me to do?

BRITON 1: You could ask God to help us.

BRITON 2: You could tell Rome not to abandon us.

GERMANUS: Rome has troubles of her own just now. Her empire is falling apart.

BRITON 4: And what has it left us? Churches to pray in.

BRITON 2: Hypocausts to hide in.

BRITON 3: Baths to drown ourselves in.

BRITON 4: Roads to speed our enemies towards us.

BRITON 3: Besides, it's too late for that. The Saxons are ashore already and banded together with the Scots and the Picts.

*(Points towards rear of auditorium)*

They're coming this way, right now! And they'll kill every last one of us when they get here!

GERMANUS: Peace! Peace! Calm yourselves. Coming from over yonder, you say? Well, then, I shall tell you what to do, and if God wills it, you will drive off the invaders.

*(He goes to blackboard and begins to draw)*

They will come from here, you say, in the east. I want you to go to meet them in the great valley . . . here. You know it? I want you to hide yourselves at the head of the valley.

*(He splits the group in two)*

You hide to the south side, you to the north, and you . . .

*(He turns to address the audience)*

You must range yourself along the valley sides.

BRITON 1: For an ambush, you mean?

GERMANUS: Like an ambush, yes. When the enemy come in sight, give the signal. Then I want everybody to shout.

BRITON 1: (*highly dubious*) Shout?

BRITON 2: Shout what?

BRITON 3: Boo? Peepo? Cooee?

BRITON 4: Charge!

GERMANUS: Hmmm.

(*Thinks, pacing up and down*)

BRITON 1: Death to the Saxons?

BRITON 2: Picts go home?

BRITON 3: All Scots are rubbish?

BRITON 4: Yah boo, come and get us?

GERMANUS: Hmmm.

PLANT IN AUDIENCE: Hallelujah?

GERMANUS: Just so! The very thing! Thank you. Well done. Hurry now, and do exactly as I told you.

BRITON 1: It's too late, I tell you! They're coming! See how the birds fly up. See how the smoke rises off the fields! Hear the crying on the wind!

BRITON 2: Now God help us, or we are history.

BRITON 3: Gone, like the Romans before us.

(*They dash to the edges of the stage and crouch down. Down the centre aisle from the rear of the hall come the* PICTS/SCOTS/SAXONS, *chanting. Loutish, like football hooligans*)

SAXONS: Here we come, with fire and sword:

A wolfish, unstoppable hoard.

SCOTS: Here we come from lands far flung,

Your British air in our lungs.

PICTS: Here we come, like carrion crows

Picking over Celtic bones.

ALL INVADERS: Here we come like wolves in a pack,

Blood on our swords and loot on our back.

First you cowardly Britons to kill

And then to feast and drink our fill . . .

(*A signal is flashed around the room using mirrors (if possible*))

SAXON: What was that?

(GERMANUS *takes up position centre stage and points his bishop's crook stage left*)

ALL BRITONS: (*stage left, shouting*) HALLELUJAH!

(GERMANUS *points his bishop's crook stage right*)

BRITONS: (*stage right*) HALLELUJAH!!

(GERMANUS *points at audience, prompter with card appears. Cue taped echoing shouts if possible to swell the noise*)

AUDIENCE AND ALL BRITONS: HALLELUJAH!!!

PICTS: There must be thousands of them!

SCOTS: With all the angels on their side!

SAXONS: They're all around us! Let's get out of here!

(*All* INVADERS *run! They scatter in all directions, then run out the way they came in. The* BRITONS *emerge one by one, grinning foolishly. The littlest shakes a fist after them*)

SMALLEST BRITON: And don't come back!

(*All the* BRITONS *begin to dance and congratulate each other*)

GERMANUS: (*to himself*) If only all battles were so easily won.

BRITON 1: Not a fight, but a fright and a flight! Hallelujah!

GERMANUS: If only all enemies were so easily routed. If only history would stand still and bring you no more troubles, my children. As it is . . . Ah well, enjoy your victory while you can.

(GERMANUS *exits left, unnoticed.* BRITONS *exit right, still slapping each other on the back*)

ALL BRITONS: (*variously*) Hallelujah!
  We showed them!
  Victory!     Did you hear that echo?

  (*Fade in end bars of Hallelujah Chorus to cover the
        emptying of the stage*)

# Alfred and the Cakes

## 878

*Programme note*

Though trounced at the Battle of Ashdown, the marauding Danes kept coming back, time after time. Many Saxon English abandoned the struggle to keep them out, but not King Alfred. In 878 he and a few loyal soldiers found themselves hiding out on the Isle of Atheleney in Somerset, hungry and weary, planning how to turn defeat into victory . . .

## Cast

KING ALFRED
DENEWULD, a cowherd
AGGIE, HIS WIFE
OFFICER OF THE KING
VIRGIN MARY (see below)

## Costumes

- tunics and cross-gartered leggings for the men
- apron for Aggie
- Alfred could conceal a simple crown at the beginning, but he should look as dirty and dishevelled as Denewuld

## Props

- bucket (preferably a wooden pail)
- mixing bowl and spoon
- 2 identical patty pans, one empty, one containing blackened ruins
- besom-type broom
- stool
- small table
- 'stove'
- sword for office
- purse on belt containing coins

## Special Effects

- smoke canisters are available from Stagecraft Promotions Ltd, Ashford Trading Estate, Salisbury, Wilts SP2 7HL

## Idea!

You might like to insert a 'dream scene' (while Alfred describes what happened) in which the audience witness his vision of the Virgin Mary.

# ALFRED AND THE CAKES

*A rickety table, a black cardboard box stage left, to represent a stove side-on to the audience, access from its back available from off stage. A stool or rolled-up sheepskin in front of the stove.*

(AGGIE *is whisking batter enthusiastically.* DENEWULD *is wiping clean a bucket. There is a knock*)

AGGIE: If it's a Dane, don't open.

DENEWULD: How do I know if it's a Dane unless I open?

AGGIE: Don't open it anyways. That's safest.

DENEWULD: Not very hospitable, though.

(*Goes to wings as if to open the door. Enter* ALFRED)

Good even to you, sir.

ALFRED: I wonder if I might trouble you for a night's shelter and a bite to eat. I've come a long way, and the weather has not been kind.

DENEWULD: Come in, come in and get warm by the fire. Aggie! Go and fetch the man a beaker of milk!

(*He gives her the bucket*)

ALFRED: You're very kind.

DENEWULD: These are hard times, stranger. We Saxons must help one another out. We have trouble enough from the Danes without shunning each other, eh? What's your name?

ALFRED: Alfred.

DENEWULD: Bless me! Same as the King! That makes you twice as welcome, Alfred. Aggie? Where's that milk?

AGGIE: (*sour and complaining*) I've got cakes to griddle. Don't know why he can't fetch in his own milk. Got hands, hasn't he?

(*Exit grumbling*)

DENEWULD: More hands than you've got good manners, wife. Don't mind my Aggie, sir. When she gets to heaven she'll complain about the whiteness of the laundry. Sit you down in front of the stove.

ALFRED: I ought to tell you: there is a reason why I bear the same name as the King . . .

DENEWULD: He may have had his setbacks lately, the King, but come the summer he'll be out there teaching the Danes a lesson they won't forget!

ALFRED: You see, I *am* the King.

DENEWULD: They say he's not far away from this very spot, you know? Keeping hid, building up his strength again.

ALFRED: That's right. That's what I'm doing.

DENEWULD: They say he met the Virgin Mary herself in the woods, you know, and cast down his cloak pin at her feet . . . You're what?

ALFRED: (*reaches to shake hands*) Alfred, King of Wessex. The rest of my army are bivouacked in the woods. Sorry-looking band just now, but, as you say, come the summer . . .

DENEWULD: (*covered in confusion. Kneels to kiss* KING's *hand, then leaps up again*) The King? Under my roof? I'll tell the wife! She'll make you up a bed! I'll roast a cow! Lord-a-mercy, the King in my house! Wait right here! Don't go anywhere. Don't move!

(*Exit running. Almost instantly,* AGGIE *enters from the other side of the stage carrying the pail. She slops milk into a cup but does not present it*)

AGGIE:  Well? There you are then. Don't let it get sour. I've got to get the cows in, me. No peace for the wicked – or for a married woman.

ALFRED:  (*points off stage*) Your husband just went looking for you.

AGGIE:  Why? Has he invited that lot to dinner as well? (*Nods towards the audience*)

(*Lots of business mixing and slopping cake mix bad-temperedly into the patty tin and putting it into the oven. It should be immediately removed from offstage and replaced with a tray of blackened lumps*)

If you want to make yourself useful, you can watch over the cakes while I fetch in the cows. Think you can do that? No nibbling, and don't you take your eyes off 'em, or I'll have words to say!

(*Exit* AGGIE. ALFRED *sits gazing into the oven. He reaches in as if to steal a bite*)

AGGIE:  (*from off*) No nibbling, you hear me!

ALFRED:  (*returns to watching. Yawns.*) Mustn't nod off. (*To audience*) Don't let me nod off, will you? Been marching since sun-up, and I was weary then. (*Nods*) The Virgin Mary, yes. What a day that was! Sunlight filtering through the tree tops and suddenly there she was, like a piece of blue fallen from the sky. I knew at once who she was.

(*Dozes. Audience wakes him*)

All right, all right. I just shut my eyes for a moment, to remember. I was struck dumb, I remember – couldn't speak. But when she smiled at me, my heart swelled up like . . . like one of those cakes there. Rose up, all golden inside me. There was a sweet smell in the air then, too. I recall . . .

(*Rests his head down on his knees, then curls up on his side.* DENEWULD *re-enters*)

DENEWULD: Can't seem to find . . . Ooops! He's sleeping. Mustn't disturb him. Shshsh!

(*Hushes audience. Sniffs savour of cooking cakes*)

Mmmm. At least we shall have cakes to offer him. Think of it! The King of Wessex in my house! Where is that wife of mine?

(*Exits. Smoke begins to billow out of the stove. Re-enter* AGGIE *who snatches out patty tin, holds it up to show, grabs a besom and begins laying about* ALFRED *with it*)

AGGIE: Great lazy, idle, good-for-nothing lummock! I leave you alone for as long as it takes a chicken to lay an egg, and what do you do? You burn my cakes! Great hulking fool of a wet Wednesday. What you got for brains, eh? Frogspawn? Look at that! Charcoal and ashes!

ALFRED: Help! Stop it! Don't you know who I am?

AGGIE: I know what you be. Anyone can see what you be! You be your mother's shame and your father's sorrow! You be a wet cloud looking for someone like me to rain on. What you be is . . .

(OFFICER *entering behind her, with* DENEWULD *cowering behind*)

OFFICER: The King of Wessex, son of Aethelwulf. Kin to the gods Woden, Sceaf and Geat. Protector of the Saxon cause. What shall I do with her, sire?

AGGIE: Me and my big mouth.

DENEWULD: What have you done, woman? You'll be the death of me one day. Today probably.

AGGIE: (*howls*) Owowo! Sorry sorry sorry sorry sorry sorry! Now they'll hang us both, and confiscate all the cows, and burn down this little house of ours . . . and it's all my fault! Me and my big mouth!

ALFRED: (*tries eating a burnt cake*) She's perfectly right, you know.

AGGIE: (*to audience, cringing*) Told you. Owowo!

ALFRED: I've ruined these cakes. The lady must be compensated! Aggie left me to mind her cakes, and I let them burn. She's quite right, I am a fool. What? Should I hang a woman for telling the simple truth? Here, madam. Here's recompense for the cakes, and a little something for your . . . honest and fearless nature. Now, gentlemen! Let's discuss what can be done to pull England from the fire before she burns, shall we?

(*He puts his arm round the necks of the* OFFICER *and* DENEWULD *and leads them off stage, leaving* AGGIE *holding the tray of cakes. She wanders dazedly off stage on the opposite side or down into the audience to offer them the burnt cakes*)

# Canute and the Sea

## 1020

## *Programme note*

Knut Sveinsson ruled three kingdoms: Norway, Denmark and, for twenty years, England. He was a brilliant, inspiring ruler and, according to legend, a lot less silly than most.

## Cast

KING CANUTE

8 TOADYING COURTIERS

2–6 DANCERS

## Costumes

- long bath robe for Canute
- circlet crown
- fancy shoes and elaborate après-ski hats for the courtiers
- leotards in grey and/or blue for the dancers

## Props

- throne
- 1, 2 or 3 × 10-metre strips of gauzy nylon material or parachute silk, greenish-grey.

## Special Effects

- sea surf and seagulls pre-recorded (optional)

## Idea!

Children might like to improvise plays based on other scenes from Canute's life: e.g. Canute turning the monks of Ely into eels; digging a canal to bypass London Bridge.

# CANUTE AND THE SEA

*Sound effect of the sea breaking on the shore, fades to silence. A high-backed chair stands centre stage.*

*(Enter* CANUTE *in a bath robe and plain circlet crown, followed by his* TOADYING COURTIERS *fawning and creeping and being generally servile)*

CANUTE:  *(casual)* What is the weather doing this morning?

1ST TOADY:  Ah! The sun was so eager to see Your Majesty that it leaped into the sky!

2ND TOADY:  It was so glad to see you well, Your Majesty, that it beams with joy!

CANUTE:  *(looks at the audience as if to say 'See what I'm up against?')* And have any letters come?

3RD TOADY: Your kingdom is so blissfully contented, Your Majesty, that no one has found a need to write.

CANUTE:  Not even any word from the Saxons?

4TH TOADY: At the thought of the mighty King Canute, they tremble too much either to speak or write!

CANUTE:  *(looks at audience again for sympathy)* What's for breakfast?

5TH TOADY: The birds of heaven vie among themselves, Your Majesty, to lay eggs befitting your gracious palate. This morning the chickens were awarded the privilege.

CANUTE:  I only asked what was for breakfast. *(Thinking aloud to himself)* What should I wear to greet the French ambassador, I wonder?

6TH TOADY:  Whatever you wear, Your Majesty, you will outshine that foreign popinjay and all other men. It is not the clothes but the man inside them who makes—

CANUTE: (*interrupting*) Do you think I'm entirely stupid?

(*Bewildered pause*)

7TH TOADY: The sages of Europe marvel, Your Majesty, at your wisdom.

CANUTE: I know. And I dare say I could cross swords with the moon and win?

8TH TOADY: Oh, no doubt of it, my lord King!

CANUTE: And command the sea itself to do my bidding?

1ST TOADY: The seven oceans, my lord, would be honoured to serve you.

CANUTE: Then take hold of that throne – you – you – and you! – and carry it down to the beach. Let's just find out whether you're right, shall we?

(*Exit* CANUTE *stage right*)

ALL COURTIERS: (*look at each other in alarm*) Whoops.

(*They struggle off, stage right, with the throne.*)

CANUTE *enters, followed by the* COURTIERS *still struggling with the throne. They place it centre stage. Sea sound effect rises.* DANCERS *in blue and grey hold either end of long gauzy blue strips, gently rippling them at floor level at the very front of the stage*)

CANUTE: Set it down here. Is the tide rising or falling, Magnusson?

1ST TOADY: Rising, Your Majesty.

CANUTE: It *was* rising, you mean, surely.

(*He sits in the throne and holds out both hands*)

Hold off, Sea! I, King Knut Sveinsson of England, Norway and Denmark say you shall not rise today!

(*The* COURTIERS *stand about grinning, their grins becoming more and more 'fixed', their worry more and more obvious*)

Stay back, I say, thou great wet thing! I, Canute command it!

(*As the scene progresses, the* DANCERS *billow the blue gauze gradually higher and higher, so that it appears to be wetting everyone's feet, knees, thighs etc. Occasional waves are higher than the rest, and at these the* COURTIERS *cry out as if splashed by spray, flapping their hands and trying to keep one foot at a time out of the water.* COURTIERS *on either side of the throne can 'rock' it*)

O unruly and uppish monster! Do you defy me? Do you dare to invade my kingdom?

1ST TOADY:  I really think, Your Majesty . . . It's not quite safe to . . .

CANUTE:  Stay back, I said! But you told me I was more powerful than the sea.

3RD TOADY:  Of course you are, my lord, but . . . Oh, my shoes!

5TH TOADY:  Oh, my hose!

7TH TOADY:  Oh, my goodness.

1ST TOADY:  It is very c-c-cold, Your Majesty.

CANUTE:  (*stands up on his throne, bunching his fists melodramatically*) Scurvy ocean! I see that you have no proper respect for an all-powerful king! I see we must wrestle hand-to-hand!

ALL COURTIERS:  (*making a grab at his legs to restrain him*) No, Your Majesty!

CANUTE:  (*with exaggerated amazement*) Do you mean to say I am *not* all-powerful? Do you mean to say that the winds and waves don't obey God's anointed king?

2ND TOADY: Er . . .

4TH TOADY: We . . .

6TH TOADY: Ah . . .

CANUTE: No? Then in future, I'll thank you not to treat me as if I were something between a god and a fairground magician. Kings are no different from ordinary men. They need the help and advice of the men around them. They do not need flattery and lies. Do I make myself clear?

ALL COURTIERS: Perfectly, Your Majesty.

*(A wave breaks right over their heads)*

Owowo!

*(They stumble off stage, arms away from their sides, legs apart, shaking their feet, as if soaked to the skin. The roar of the ocean continues, the* DANCERS *taking over the area left vacant by the actors)*

# Lady Godiva's Shameless Ride

## about 1050

*Programme note*

Godiva, wife of the Earl of Mercia, was renowned for her charitable acts. But when her husband imposed yet another tax on the sorely pressed people of Coventry, no one guessed what Godiva would do in order to change his mind.

## Cast

EARL LEOFRIC

LADY GODIVA

TOM HENNY

CHORUS comprising: elderly WIDOW

| | |
|---|---|
| WOMAN WITH BABE-IN-ARMS | FISHMONGER |
| BARBER | SOLDIER |
| GOSSIP | |

optional PERCUSSIONIST to make clip-clop noises (see below)

## Costumes

• wig for Godiva (if she does not have long blonde hair already)
• white butcher's apron
• workman's apron
• perhaps a steeple hat
• cloak for Leofric

## Props

• big book and quill pen
• goblet
• chorus props are best 'pretend'; cut-throat razor, baby, walking-stick, rifle, etc.
• eye-patch

## Special Effects

• pre-recorded sound of horse's hooves or a percussion instrument which will produce the same sound

## Idea!

If the rhythm is made very emphatic, the choral verses will be easier to learn and easier to synchronise. They may need 'conducting', like music.

# LADY GODIVA'S SHAMELESS RIDE

*The* CHORUS *are already at the back of the stage, their backs turned to the audience.* LEOFRIC *is seated stage front, adding up figures in a large book.*

(GODIVA *brings him a cup of wine*)

LEOFRIC: There! A nice round figure!

GODIVA: (*she looks over his shoulder*) It is a very large figure.

LEOFRIC: A useful sum. It will come in useful.

GODIVA: What does it represent?

LEOFRIC: It's the sum I shall raise from my new tax on Coventry.

GODIVA: A new tax?

LEOFRIC: Ah now, Godiva, don't pretend to understand economics. You confine yourself to counting threads in your needlework.

GODIVA: But Leofric – a new tax? Is it lower than the last? Oh, God will bless you, if you reduce Coventry's taxes!

LEOFRIC: Reduce them? Don't be foolish, woman. This is a new levy on top of the old. Some way to go before we reach the bottom of that barrel!

GODIVA: But Leofric! It's all they can do to pay now! Every day I hear stories of hardship and suffering . . .

LEOFRIC: Stories! Ooo, yes. They're great ones for telling stories about why they can't pay. Don't believe a word of it, wife. There's plenty more milk to be had from that particular cow.

GODIVA: But they're not cows, husband! They're people! They're hard-working, struggling people beset by your taxes and levies and fines and tolls. Oh Leofric, please! The Bible tells us to help the poor!

LEOFRIC: The Bible tells us to work hard and pay our taxes. Sentimental pish tosh! You are so gullible, wife. If you didn't squander my money on your lame ducks and hopeless causes, I might not be put to raising taxes. Oh, I've seen you! Giving silver to beggars in the street, and your clothes to ragamuffin sluts at the door.

GODIVA: I only give away what's mine! If you really need this money, I'll give it to you out of my own inheritance.

LEOFRIC: Your own? I'll have you know, madam, your money is already mine for the taking. And I do not please to use my own money to pay what the people of Coventry owe me. Not another word. If I want, I shall tax Coventry till the sweat runs from its eyeballs.

*(He slaps shut his book and gets up to go. He has almost gone when . . .)*

GODIVA: No!

*(He stops and turns, supercilious. She crosses to him and kneels down)*

On my knees, I beg you, husband. I've never contradicted you before, but this is wrong. Don't do it. You can't know the suffering it would cause! For God's sake, if not for mine, don't hound the people for more taxes!

LEOFRIC: Silence, woman. Get up. Don't make a spectacle of yourself. What business is it of yours if I tax Coventry till its bricks bleed?

*(He crosses the stage as if to leave another way.*

*GODIVA* still *kneels*)

GODIVA:  Well, then, if you won't be ashamed, I must be shamed for you. My money may be yours, but, I think you'll agree, my body is my own? Withdraw this latest tax . . . or I shall ride naked through the streets of Coventry in token of the people you have left naked to wind and rain!

LEOFRIC:  (*long pause then he laughs uproariously*) You? The virtuous Lady Godiva, wife of the Earl of Mercia? Ride naked through the streets? You'd die of shame and I'd die laughing!

(*Exit* LEOFRIC *laughing loudly.* GODIVA *exits opposite side. The* CHORUS *of townspeople turn to face the audience*)

GOSSIP:  Have you heard what they're saying?

FISHMONGER:  I heard it down the fish market. Everyone's talking about it.

WIDOW:  I heard it in church! The vicar announced it after morning service. It must be true!

BARBER:  I was so shook up when I heard, I nearly cut a customer's throat!

WOMAN WITH BABY:  It's never true! It can't be true! Not Lady Godiva! Not that gentle, God-fearing lady!

SOLDIER:  Ride through the streets, naked? Make a spectacle of herself? And be stared at like some dancing bear.

TOM HENNY:  (*salacious*) Bare's the word. Bare as the day her mother bore her. Now won't that be a sight for sore eyes, eh?

WIDOW:  What if it were my daughter?

FISHMONGER:  What if it were my wife?

BARBER:  What if it were my sister?

TOM HENNY: If it were your sister, no one would bother to look – but Godiva! (*wolf whistles*)

FISHMONGER: She's doing this for us! To shame that grasping husband of hers. He shouldn't let her!

BARBER: He can't stop her.

(*Pause for thought*)

WIDOW: *We* could stop her. Leastways, we could stop her being shamed.

WOMAN WITH BABY: (*catching on*) I don't think I'll be going out tomorrow.

WIDOW: I don't think I'll be opening my shutters.

FISHMONGER: I don't think I shall be setting up my stall in the market place.

BARBER: I don't think I'll be opening my shop.

(*They all turn and look expectantly at* TOM)

TOM HENNY: (*sneeringly*) Oh yeah?

BARBER: Yes, Tom. (*To audience*) We'll none of us shame the lady by looking, will we? . . . I said, will we?

TOM HENNY: (*grudgingly, glaring at the audience*) Oh, all right, then. Have it your way. Killjoys.

(*Pauses at edge of stage and looks shiftily around, grinning, rubbing hands together. Enter* LEOFRIC. *The* CHORUS *turn their backs. He paces up and down, anxiously wringing his hands*)

LEOFRIC: She won't, will she? She wouldn't, would she? Suffer those filthy curs and fishwives to stare at her? Get herself talked about in ale-houses? Shame me and herself in public? Make us a laughing stock? She wouldn't, would she? She won't . . . (*To audience*) will she?

(*Exit* LEOFRIC. *Recorded sound of horse's hooves clip-*

*clopping slowly, getting louder. The* CHORUS *of townspeople on stage turn, and advance to front of stage,
chanting louder and louder)*

ALL:  Lady Godiva, Lady Godiva,
Pale horse and paler rider
Only her lonely shadow beside her:
Lady Godiva, Lady Godiva.

Modesty burning like coals inside her,
Thinking that thousands will throng to deride her
Saddened that such a small wish was denied her.
Lady Godiva, Lady Godiva.

Only her flaxen hair to hide her
Naked truth in a naked rider
Our friend, our help, our sole provider,
Lady Godiva, Lady Godiva.

*(They mime shutting their shutters. All cover their eyes
with both hands. Almost shouting now)*

No woman look, and no man neither,
Cursed be the beady eyes that spy her:
Not so much as a weaving spider
Shall steal a look at Lady Godiva!

*(They turn their backs again and return upstage, repeat-
ing the first verse, but very softly. Meanwhile,* TOM *tip-
toes on stage)*

TOM HENNY:  That's what they think. I wouldn't miss this
entertainment for a mouthful of new teeth! I'll stay
indoors, all right. But doors were made with keyholes,
and keyholes were made for spying. I'm going to look my
fill and who's going to stop me. Eh? Who's going to
know?

*(He kneels down and makes a keyhole out of finger
and thumb, to peep through. The clip-clopping gets*

*louder and louder.* LEOFRIC *bursts on to the stage holding out a cloak. He offers it, as if to someone at rear of auditorium)*

LEOFRIC: (*calling*) Don't do this, Godiva! Don't do this to me! This rabble aren't worth it! Nothing is worth it! Please! Cover yourself up!

TOM HENNY: She's coming. I hear the horse. Market day, and yet there's not a sound. Not a single shout. Not a rattling cart. No one about. Just those horse's hooves coming closer and closer.

LEOFRIC: Market day, and not a soul anywhere. Where are they all? Sweaty, gawping, foul-mouthed, evil-minded rabble? Not here? Indoors? Every window barred, every shutter closed. They've turned their backs. They've shut their eyes. How they must love her, these have-nothing, no-hope beggars.

(*Remains at edge of stage, amazed*)

TOM HENNY:  Lady Godiva, Lady Godiva,
Sweet as pickled eggs and cider.
What I'd give to ride behind yer.
Eyes open wide. Eyes open wider:
Soon be seeing you, Lady Godiva . . .

(*The* CHORUS *make a loud 'hoowoo', as of rushing wind*)

Aaah!

(*He claps his hands to his eye and rolls around in agony*)

Grit in my eye! Blown through the lock! My eye! My eye!
I'm blinded! Aaah!

(*Stumbles off stage. The* CHORUS *shout after him, then
exit opposite side*)

CHORUS:  Peeping Tom!

(GODIVA *enters from the other side of the stage, dressed
as before*)

GODIVA:  Well, husband? You may think worse of me,
after today, but I hope you think better of Coventry. Did
you see how the people behaved?

LEOFRIC:  I saw.

GODIVA:  They stayed inside their houses.

LEOFRIC:  They refused to shame you.

GODIVA:  Not one looked at me.

LEOFRIC:  And now, neither can I. I'm too ashamed.

GODIVA:  I've told you before: Coventry is full of kind,
honourable people.

LEOFRIC:  Who love you dearly. Almost as much as I do
. . . It's all right, Godiva. Before you ask, I shan't impose
the new taxes. In fact I shall halve the taxes I take from

Coventry . . .

GODIVA:  Oh Leofric! That's wonderful!

LEOFRIC:  I'll tax Chester, instead.

> (LEOFRIC *hastily exits, laughing*)

GODIVA:  (*exit protesting, in pursuit of* LEOFRIC) Leofric? You don't really mean that? Was that a joke? Leofric? Husband? Tell me that was a joke . . .

TOM HENNY:  (*enters wearing an eye-patch*) Lady Godiva, Lady Godiva,
Devil take and devil grind her!
See my permanent reminder
Of that flaxen-haired rider?
Devil take your kind, Godiva!

> (*The* CHORUS *jostle him off stage*)

# Who Killed Red Rufus?

## 1100

*Programme note*

William II won the English crown by making promises he did not keep. He was loathed for his cruelty and sacrilege. So what happened one summer morning while he was staying at Winchester?

## Cast

WILLIAM RUFUS (red-headed)
WILLIAM TIREL, his huntmaster
2 COURTIERS
PAGE
CHILD
ARROWSMITH
3–5 TREES who can sing
RECORDER PLAYER
2 WOODSMEN

## Costumes

- red wig for Rufus, if necessary
- crown
- rich cloak
- less splendid cloak for courtier
- raggy clothing for woodsmen
- leafy wreaths for trees

## Props

- medium-sized toy dog
- small stirrup (e.g. off a rocking horse) on its leather
- very large stirrup on its leather
- at least 2 bows
- quiver containing arrows
- parchment letter
- shortened arrow for Rufus to palm
- wheelbarrow
- artificial blood (optional)

## Special Effects

- pre-recorded twang and thud of arrow being fired

## Songs

These are all from *The National Song Book*, published by Boosey & Hawkes and are out of copyright so long as the music is not reproduced.

# WHO KILLED RED RUFUS?

*Music is used here to set a woodland scene. The* TREES *remain on stage throughout, observing the action. Give plenty of time to their opening, and leave several seconds between tunes: slow, melancholy, mystical.*

RECORDER *plays opening line of 'The Holly and the Ivy'*

1ST TREE: (*sings*) The ash grove how graceful, how plainly 'tis speaking.

2ND TREE: Oh the oak and the ash and the bonny ivy tree . . .

1ST TREE: The wind through its branches . . .

3RD TREE: Oh, the Holly and the Ivy!

1ST TREE: . . . has language for me.

(*A chair is brought on, stage right, to imply an indoor scene as* RECORDER *repeats opening refrain of 'The Holly and the Ivy'. Enter* RUFUS *in a rage, shaking dog over his head. He is followed by* CHILD *in tears, reaching up for the dog*)

RUFUS: This dog . . . this dog . . . This dog has four legs! Why does this dog have four legs? Can somebody tell me why this dog has four legs?

CHILD: Please, Your Majesty! Please don't hurt him! Please!

RUFUS: Tirel, you're my huntmaster: can you explain to me why this dog has four legs? Isn't there a law banning all dogs from my forest? This is my forest. I come here to hunt. Dogs hunt, Tirel. Isn't that true? Dogs hunt. That's why no dogs. No dogs that can run, at least. No dogs unless they've had one leg cut off. So! Can you explain this to me, then?

CHILD: No! no! Don't cut Tray's leg off. Don't hurt him!

TIREL: Small dog, Your Majesty? Your Majesty permitted dogs small enough to pass through a stirrup.

RUFUS: Well? Well? Where's the stirrup? Show me! Does this look like a small dog to you?

(TIREL *pulls the standard stirrup, on its leather, from his belt and holds it up. It is patently too small for the dog to pass through*)

Try it! Go on! Try it, by all means! . . . And if it doesn't fit through . . . *trim it till it does.*

CHILD: No! No! Please!

(TIREL *seems obliged to obey but hesitates, glancing at the* CHILD *and at the cloaked* COURTIER 1 *standing closely beside him. Enter* PAGE *stage right with arrows.* RUFUS *has to turn to take the arrows and while he does so,* TIREL *passes the stirrup swiftly sideways to the cloaked man who returns a much, much larger stirrup*)

PAGE: The arrowsmith has delivered your new arrows, Your Majesty.

RUFUS: Ah yes! My new arrows! High time, too. I should be out there hunting, not waiting upon arrowsmiths and dogs! Well? Does the dog fit through? Does it?

(*To* RUFUS's *disgust, the dog fits through the large stirrup and the* CHILD *runs off cuddling it*)

I should have made all dogs outlaws, and hanged them. Better still, I should burn down every village in the forest. The peasants are worse vermin than their dogs . . .

(*Enter* PAGE *with letter and King's cloak*)

PAGE: A letter is come from the Abbey, Your Majesty.

RUFUS: (*busy putting on his cloak*) Read it to me, Tirel.

TIREL: (*reads*) 'The brothers of Winchester beg and beseech Your Majesty to be hourly on thy guard. One of our fellowship hath dreamed a dream this night. He dreamed a woman knelt before the throne of Christ, speaking these words: "Remove from the necks of thy people, O Lord, the yoke (hesitates nervously) *which is William Rufus.*"'

(RECORDER *repeats opening refrain of 'The Holly and the Ivy'*)

RUFUS: Well? What are you gaping at? It's a threat. I get them all the time. They hate me. They all hate me: the Church, because I said I'd change my religion if it paid; the peasants because I maim and hang them . . . Round here, they say even the trees hate William Rufus. What of it? Should I be afraid of trees? Or monks? Or peasants? Ooo. See me tremble.

(*He snatches the letter and screws it up*)

Well? Are we hunting today or not? Here you are, Tirel. Don't say I never give you anything.

(*He gives two arrows to* TIREL *and puts the rest into his quiver. Exit all stage right.* RECORDER *repeats opening refrain of 'The Holly and the Ivy'.* RUFUS, TIREL *and* COURTIERS *reappear wearing cloaks,* RUFUS, *half-crouching, stalking a deer, pointing stage left with bow.* TIREL *is also carrying a bow. The fatal arrow is already in* RUFUS's *hand*)

There it is! Are you all blind as well as stupid? A big fallow buck. Tirel, go downwind and drive it towards me.

(TIREL *exits stage left*)

That's it! That's it! Drive him this way! He's mine! The kill's mine!

(*Noise of twanging bowstring off stage.* RUFUS *drops his bow and crashes to the ground, back to audience. He grips the arrow by its head and holds his fist against his chest, as if just shot in the heart. Rolls on to his back and dies at length*)

COURTIER 1: He's dead.

COURTIER 2: Stone dead.

(*Re-enter* TIREL, *breathless*)

TIREL: What happened? An accident? An ambush? Who fired? Did you see who shot the arrow?

(*The* COURTIERS *stare at him*)

COURTIER 1: It's your arrow.

COURTIER 2: It's a lot like the one he gave you this morning.

TIREL: No! No! You don't really think . . . I didn't shoot him! I was over there. I never . . .

COURTIER 1: I believe you.

COURTIER 2: Nobody would blame you.

TIREL: Won't blame me, no. But they'll hang me. Someone's got to hang for it. And I can't prove . . . I'm going! I'm getting out of the country before anyone lays this at my door! But tell them! Tell them, it wasn't me!

(*Exit* TIREL, *running*)

COURTIER 2: What do we do? Should we move him? Where should we take him?

COURTIER 1: (*spits*) Let him lie where he is, or let the devil take him. He wanted the forest to himself while he lived. Let him have it now he's dead. Tirel's right. Blood sticks. You were never here. I was never here. We never saw a thing.

(*They exit, leaving* RUFUS *where he is.* RECORDER *repeats opening refrain of 'The Holly and the Ivy'. Enter two* WOODSMEN *with a wheelbarrow*)

WOODSMAN 1: Look, Will. What's been a-doin' 'ere?'

WOODSMAN 2: Foul play by the looks. Some unfortunate soul come 'twixt bow and target.

WOODSMAN 1: (*looking more closely*) This is no unfortunate. See that red 'air? This is Red Rufus, that's who. The King hisself!

(*They both gasp and gaze down at the King for a long time*)

WOODSMAN 2: Well, happy day. Couldn't 'appen to a nicer fellow.

WOODSMAN 1: Good riddance to bad rubbish, yeah. Brought misery to these parts like a haywain bringin' hay. I'd give a shilling to him as did this.

WOODSMAN 2: If you 'ad a shilling.

(*They continue to gaze at the body*)

WOODSMAN 1: We might get a shilling if we was to cart him off some place. The Abbey or some place. What say?

WOODSMAN 2: Might at that. The hogs'll eat him, if we leave him 'ere. Let's put him in the barrow and take him into Winchester.

WOODSMAN 1: Him'll mess up the barrow, all that blood.

WOODSMAN 2: (*gives this grave consideration*) Worth it for a shilling.

(*They get* RUFUS *into the wheelbarrow, as they speak*)

WOODSMAN 1: Worth it for the joy it'll bring to folk to see Red Rufus dead in a barrow. Though I doubt anyone'll give 'im Christian burial when we get him there. Him being such a godless devil. Wonder who did for 'im?

WOODSMAN 2: The 'and of God, if you ask me. The blessed 'and of God – and not a minute too soon.

(*Exit both pushing the wheelbarrow. The* TREES *repeat the refrains they sang/played at the beginning*)

# The Troubadour Rescues his King

## 1193

## Programme note

On his way home from the Crusades, King Richard I was taken prisoner by the Duke of Austria and held, as a valuable political pawn, in secret captivity. Legend credits his minstrel, Blondel, with tracking him down. Here is a pantomime version of the well-loved story.

## Cast

RICHARD THE LIONHEART

BLONDEL

PRINCE JOHN

5 OR 6 SOLDIERS

4 OR 5 COURTIERS

## Costumes

- large silly crown for Richard (e.g. tea cosy)
- Prince John should be dressed in black, including gloves
- tabards for soldiers
- lots of knee boots, curl-toed slippers, bright colours, tabards, tights

## Props

- lute (or guitar), badly out of tune
- sword for at least one soldier
- ball and chain (very light football)
- large garish handkerchief

## Special Effects

- recording of 'The Pearl Fisher' duet

## Idea!

Get the children to discuss the traditions of pantomime: e.g. transformations, rhyming script, dames, cross-dressing, villains entering from the left, heroes from the right. This last dates back to the earliest mystery plays when the Hill of Heaven stood stage right, the Mouth of Hell stage left.

# THE TROUBADOUR RESCUES HIS KING

*To be acted in pantomime style. On stage an upright screen stands askew, with a barred prison window cut in it.*

(BLONDEL *enters carrying a guitar*)

BLONDEL: Good day! Good day! My name's Blondel
The King of England's best minstrel.
What better life than mine, to sing
And play for England's greatest king!
We sing duets: the perfect pair.
I'm Ginger to his Fred Astaire.
So welcome please, with all your heart,
Richard, known as Lionheart!

(*Enter* RICHARD, *skipping, waving handkerchief, wearing big, silly crown*)

RICHARD: Thank you, thank you, dear Blondel.
Hail and, sadly, then farewell.
Ladies, teachers, gentlemen:
I'm off on my Crusades again!
Off to the hot and Holy Land
To earn my place in heaven's band.

BLONDEL: O then, strike up a joyful paeon

For Richard, known as Coeur de Lion!

(*Exit* RICHARD *while* BLONDEL *waves, sheds a tear then sits down on the edge of the stage and tunes his lute. Enter* PRINCE JOHN, *all in black, collar raised furtively, long low strides*)

JOHN: I'm bad Prince John, King Richard's brother,
The one not so much loved by Mother.
May no good come of Dick's adventure.
A pox upon your primogeniture!
Well travel far and travel long:
I'll wear the crown while you are gone!
You can boo and hiss for all you're worth:
'Cos brains count more than royal birth.

(*Goes to leave stage left, pauses at edge of stage to confide to audience*)

It's being ambitious
That makes me vicious.
BLONDEL: Alas, alack and well-a-day!
My master Dick has gone astray!
His home-bound ship was lost at sea
But did our Richard drown? Not he!

(RICHARD *enters wearing a false joke disguise – glasses + nose + beard*)

He travelled on from town to city
Concealing his identity –
Disguised that regal handsome brow.

(RICHARD *is unmasked by* SOLDIERS *and bundled into the 'prison cell', with ball and chain round his ankle*)

They caught him, still. (I can't think how.)

(*enter* SOLDIERS *crossing the stage one behind the other, one hand on the one in front, like Flanagan and Allen*)

ALL SOLDIERS: We seek him here. We seek him there.
But we can't find him anywhere.
No one writes to ask for ransom.
Where's our Dick, so brave and handsome?

JOHN: (*to soldiers*) What, Richard lost? Well, what a pity.
Must have died in capti-*vi*ty.
You've done enough you can't do more.

Poor Richard's dead on foreign shores.
(*aside*)Alas, alack and fiddle-de-dee.
The King is dead, so long live *me*!

(*As before, goes to exit, rubbing hands with glee; pauses
to confide*)

It's having to deal with peasants
That makes me so unpleasant.

(*Exit* JOHN)

RICHARD:  For such as me, this place is hell,
This pestilential prison cell.
Nought to do and nought to see
And no Blondel for company.
Oh, must I live my life out here?
Day by week by month by year?
Why does no one come and find me
Oh to put this woe behind me!
BLONDEL:  Fear not, my poor, unhappy master!
I will save you from disaster.
Pledged to find you, I, Blondel
Will search each fort and citadel
Until I find the King my friend
And bring his ordeal to an end!

(*Begins searching the stage*)

ALL SOLDIERS:  (*change arms and cross stage in the other
direction, as before*)

We seek him here. We seek him there.
But we can't find him anywhere.
We would gladly pay a ransom
For dear Dick so brave and handsome!

BLONDEL:  I have sniffed and scoured about
And this is what I've winkled out.
There's someone held in closest secret
In this castle's oubliette.

No one's ever seen his face.
None's allowed inside the place.

(*Whispers at audience, as* COURTIERS *enter*)

I'll join the owner's entourage
Using my lute for camouflage.
I'll ply my trade and while I sing
Discover if I've found the King.
Well? Every door's an open door
To a skilful troubadour.

(*Begins strumming. Coughs. Looks for the right note*)

Me-me-me-meee!

RICHARD: I know that voice? It can't be! Yes!
It's Julio Iglesias!
No, no. Blondel! It is! My man! . . .

But how to show him where I am?

(*Picks up ball and chain under one arm. Climbs on chair. Coughs. Looks for right note*)

Me-me-me-meee. (*Clasps lapel with other hand*)

(RICHARD *and* BLONDEL *mime to pre-recorded 'Pearl Fisher's Duet'*)

BLONDEL: (*to audience*) I said we were good.

(*As* SOLDIERS *speak,* RICHARD *is freed from prison and they wave little Union Jacks*)

ALL SOLDIERS: We searched and searched like anything
But loyal Blondel found the King.
He brought home word, and soon a ransom
Bought the life of bold and handsome
Richard Coeur de Lion!

(*Enter* PRINCE JOHN, *raging*)

PRINCE JOHN: Foiled again! Oh spit and curses!
Foiled by Blondel and his verses!
Hell and blazing botheration!
Cancel my lovely coronation!

(*To audience, in going, as before*)

You'll be sorry! You won't hiss
When Richard meets his nemesis.
Songs and minstrels! They make me sick.
You're heartily welcome to Lionheart Dick!

# Robert the Bruce
# and the Spider
## 1306

*Programme note*

Hounded and dispossessed by the English, Robert the Bruce was on the brink of despair when he took shelter one night in a ruined hut on the island of Rathlin. He had just lost six battles in a row. Surely now he must admit defeat and abandon his claim to the Scottish crown?

## Cast

ROBERT THE BRUCE

CHORUS OF 7 (variable)

3 SPIDER OPERATORS

## Costumes

- ragged tunic and leggings + ragged blanket
- chorus – no costumes necessary

## Props

- sword for Bruce
- various weapons lying on the stage between members of the chorus
- spider on pole (see diagram)
- pale-coloured screen
- a large, loopy spider's web of 'Wanted' notices: ROBERT BRUCE: LOST, STOLEN OR STRAYED
- prompt cards for audience: COME ON, SPIDER!; DON'T GIVE UP NOW!; YOU CAN DO IT!; ONE MORE TRY!

## Idea!

There is good drama fun to be had from discussing the different ways the word 'Oh!' can be said.

# ROBERT THE BRUCE AND THE SPIDER

*The chorus sit along the front of the stage. A three-sided structure like a bus shelter with a bench seat within it occupies the centre of the stage. Behind this stands the spider operator(s). Enter* BRUCE, *clutching a holey blanket round him, dripping wet. Nice big gaps between cries of 'Oh!'*

BRUCE: Oh! (cold) Oh! (fed up) Oh! (rubbing his aching back) Oh! (exasperation) Oh! (whimpering) Oh! (howling) (sits down) Ow! (Picks up a sharp stone off bench and chucks it angrily) Oh! (Mopish. Sits, head in hands)

CHORUS 1: Robert the Bruce.

CHORUS 2: King of Scotland.

CHORUS 3: For what it's worth.

CHORUS 4: The English are looking for him. They have put up wanted notices all over the countryside.

CHORUS 5: Robert Bruce: lost, stolen or strayed!

CHORUS 6: Every day another friend of his is captured.

CHORUS 7: Another member of his family is hanged.

CHORUS 1: Six battles he has fought with the English.

BRUCE: Six battles!

CHORUS 2: And every one of them lost.

CHORUS 3: So now he's on the run.

CHORUS 4: Sheltering under branches and in caves.

CHORUS 5: Eating rabbits, berries and fish.

CHORUS 6: Feeling sorry for himself.

CHORUS 7: Wondering whether to give himself up.

ALL CHORUS: Then, one night, on the island of Rathlin ...
(*The* CHORUS *turn, so as to watch what happens.* BRUCE *lies down on the bench, which is too short, and wriggles around trying to get comfortable. He ends up flat on his back, head hanging off the end of the bench. The* SPIDER OPERATOR *swings the giant spider round the end of the screen to hang suspended over* BRUCE)

BRUCE: Oooergh.

(*The* SPIDER *swings to and fro. (It does not matter how silly it looks)*)

BRUCE: It's trying to get a web started. Trying to get a thread of gossamer from that side to the other.

(*Lots more tries by the spider*)

What perseverance! What determination! Will it never give up? That spider's even more of a failure than I am. Still it keeps trying. It just doesn't know when it's beaten. Too far, little spider! Build smaller, why don't you? Scuttle away into a corner, like Robert the Bruce, and weave there. No. On it goes. Single-minded. Tireless. Its little heart set on building a giant empire.

(*The* SPIDER *stops at one end of its arc*)

Ah, are you tired now? That makes two of us. Tell you what! If you make one more try – if you succeed – then by all that's holy, so will I!

(*He leans up on one elbow, to watch*)

CHORUS 1: Will it?

CHORUS 2: Won't it?

CHORUS 3: Will the spider give up?

CHORUS 4: Or will the spider fail?

CHORUS 5: Suddenly the Bruce's future is bound up in gossamer twine.

CHORUS 6: His future depends on this small ball of leggy blackness.

CHORUS 7: Scotland's fate is hanging on a thread!

(*Members of the* CHORUS *hold up prompt cards to the audience and encourage them to shout out:*

*COME ON, SPIDER!*
*DON'T GIVE UP NOW!*
*YOU CAN DO IT!*
*ONE MORE TRY!*

*Then they drum on the stage with their hands in approximation of a drumroll. The* SPIDER *swings to the other end of the arc and stays there.* BRUCE *springs up triumphant, fists in the air*)

BRUCE: I can do it! I can drive the English out of

Scotland. I can wear the crown that's rightfully mine! And if I do . . .

(*Looks round at the spider. A huge web flops down over back wall.*)

When I do, I shall make pilgrimage to Jerusalem and give thanks. This I swear, O Lord!

(*Looks upwards and raises a clenched fist. Then freezes*)

CHORUS 1: His luck did not change.

CHORUS 2: His little brother was hanged by the English.

CHORUS 3: His wife and sister were swung over the walls of Kildrummie Castle in wooden cages, like wild beasts.

CHORUS 4: When he gave his call to arms, the people were too terrified to answer.

CHORUS 5: (*standing up*) But now there was no stopping him.

CHORUS 6: (*standing up*) No running away.

CHORUS 7: (*standing up*) The Bruce had a new motto.

CHORUS 1: (*standing up*) If at first you don't succeed.

CHORUS 1 AND 2: Try!

CHORUS 1, 2 AND 3: Try!

ALL CHORUS: Try again!

(BRUCE *draws sword and adopts a grand heroic pose centre stage front, addressing the audience*)

BRUCE: If any man of you is not ready for either victory or death, let him leave now!

(*The* CHORUS *all draw imaginary swords and follow him, roaring, off stage*)

ALL: Conquer or die! Conquer or die! Conquer or die!

# 'Oss! Oss! Wee Oss!'

## 1347

### Programme note

No sooner had the men of Padstow set sail to take part in the siege of Calais than French troops raided the little undefended Cornish fishing port. But they had not reckoned with Padstow's most famous inhabitant.

## Cast

AT LEAST 5 WIVES
URSULA BIRDHOOD, a good witch
OBBY OSS, the Padstow hobbyhorse
at least 5 FRENCH SOLDIERS
A SUBTITLER
DRUMMER, off stage

## Costumes

- long drab skirts over flounced red petticoats
- striped French T-shirts or jerseys
- shako-type hats, even berets (optional)
- Obby Oss costume (see picture on page 79)
- red and white neckerchiefs worn as headscarves.

## Props

- (optional) cutlasses
- drum
- flipchart on stand, ready captioned with the necessary translations, each on a separate sheet

## Special Effects

- boatless rowing calls for practice, strong legs and thick trousers. The rowers sit with their legs over the top of the legs in front and bounce along on their bottoms

## Idea!

A video of the genuine Padstow Mayday would be a big advantage in learning the words, peculiar rhythm and dance of the song, and in grasping the 'feel' of the occasion. This play is an obvious choice for a Mayday assembly.

# 'OSS! OSS! WEE OSS!'

*The* WIVES *run on stage and stand on tiptoe, facing the back of the stage, waving their headscarves in farewell, and sniffling.*

WIFE 1: There they go!

WIFE 2: God bless them!

WIFE 3: And bring them safe home again.

ALL: Amen!

WIFE 4: It's a fearful long way to France.

WIFE 5: But think of the dancing when they come home again!

*(They turn away, comforting each other, replacing scarves. The last* WIFE *glances back and something catches her eye down 'in the bay'. She claps her hands over her mouth in horror)*

Wait! Look! Do you see! What boat is that?

*(The* WIVES *run back and peer out from under their hands. They gasp and look at one another)*

ALL: Frenchies!

WIFE 1: The Frenchies are coming here?

WIFE 2: And not a man in the town to fight them off!

WIFE 3: What are we going to do?

WIFE 4: Find Ursula! Ask Ursula Birdhood! She'll know what to do.

*(Exit* WIFE 2 *to look for* URSULA)

WIFE 1: They'll take the clothes from our presses.

WIFE 3: The cider out of our cups.

WIFE 4: The plaits off our children.

WIFE 5: What are we going to do?

(*Enter* URSULA, WIFE 2 *hurrying her*)

URSULA: What's the matter? What's the matter? Calm yourselves, ladies. No call to swallow your aprons.

WIFE 1: But the Frenchies are in the bay! And our men all gone out of Padstow!

WIFE 3: Can't you cast a hex on them, Mrs Birdhood, and magic them away? You're a witch, aren't you?

(*The other wives turn on her and shshsh her.* URSULA *is offended*)

URSULA: Maybe I am and maybe I'm not . . . But there's someone in Padstow who's more magic then me. (*Gestures*) From the shoes on his feet to the ribbons in his hair.

ALL WIVES: (*copy the gesture, bewildered*) From the shoes on his feet to the ribbons in his hair?

URSULA: Born on a Mayday morning?

ALL WIVES: The Obby Oss!

URSULA: Quite. Now go home all of you and put on your best red petticoats. Then find a drum and let's fetch out the Obby Oss from his winter sleep. I'll meet you all at Stepper Point!

WIVES: Yes. Mmmm. Right.

(*They nod, but do not move, still staring out to sea*)

URSULA: Well? What are you waiting for?

WIVES: Oh. Right!

(*Exit* WIVES)

URSULA:  Now Cornwall, shake up your bones.

Give me your bright-light magic.

Give me your tin-bone magic.

(*A throbbing drumbeat starts, off stage*)

Give me your deep-mine magic, your white-clay magic.

Give me your shine-water magic.

Up Cornwall and toss these Frenchies back to France!

(*Exit* URSULA. *The* FRENCHIES *'row' on stage, sitting as in a rowing boat, legs round the person in front and miming rowing, progressing across the stage from left to right by bottom-bouncing. The* WIVES, *meanwhile, enter in a line, clutching their shawls round them. They have put on long, red waist-petticoats. Last comes* URSULA *who turns and calls to someone lagging behind off stage*)

URSULA:  Come, old friend. Come and partner us. The Frenchies are in the bay and we've a mind to dance.

WIFE 1:  Dance? What good will that do?

WIFE 2:  Dance? With the town about to burn?

WIFE 3:  Dance? With Frenchies comes to ravish us away?

URSULA:  Dance, yes! Can't you hear the drum? Kick up your heels and show your red petticoats! See? (*Grand gesture*) The leader of the dance!

(*Enter* OBBY OSS, *rushing at the* WIVES *and making them shriek*)

URSULA:  (*sings*) Unite and unite, and let us all unite
For summer is acome unto day;
And whither we are going, we will all unite
In the merry morning of May!

(WIVES *join in hesitantly, as* URSULA *sings. They dance as they sing, spreading their petticoats*)

Where are the young men that here now should dance?
For summer is acome unto day;
Some they are in England and some they are in France,
In the merry morning of May!
Oss! Oss! Wives! Wee Oss!

(*Urging the audience to sing*) Let every soul in Padstow
sing the May Song, and we'll make it May in winter!
Unite and unite, and let us all unite
For summer is acome unto day;
And whither we are going, we will all unite
In the merry morning of May!

(*The* FRENCHIES *have, by this time, reached stage right.
Each man who speaks stands up to say his line, setting
the 'boat' rocking.* SUBTITLER *enters conspicuously with
flipchart, which she proceeds to display for the benefit of
the audience, turning the pages after each line spoken, to
display the translation*)

FRENCHIE 1: *Voilà! En haut! Le village ce n'est pas vide!*
[Look! Up there! The village isn't empty!]

FRENCHIE 2: *Qui est-ce? Quels gens?*
[Who can it be? What people?]

*Les soldats anglais! Regardez leurs gilets rouges!
Beaucoup, beaucoup de gilets-rouges!*
[English soldiers! See the red coats? Lots and lots of red-coats!]

FRENCHIE 3: *Et qu'est-ce qu'il y a au milieu? Une bête
noire qui saute, qui cabriole, que se cabre!*
[Who's that in the middle? The black beast jumping and
capering and prancing?]

FRENCHIE 4: *C'est le diable! Sans doute, c'est le diable
hors d'Infer!*

[It's the devil got loose from hell.]

EACH FRENCHIE: (*in turn*) *Le diable? Le diable?*

[The Devil??!!]

*Le diable! Le diable!*

FRENCHIE 5: *Merde!*
[Oh dear!]

URSULA: They take you for the devil, Oss. They mistake you for Old Nick himself! They think the Cornishmen can summon up the devil to fight for them! But what do we need with the devil, eh ladies? One Cornishwoman is worth a fleet of French matelots! Oss! Oss!

ALL WIVES: Wee Oss!

FRENCHIE I: *Sacré! Je vais rentrer chez moi! Je ne veux pas combattre de diable!*
[I'm off.]

FRENCHIE 2: *Allons! Quittons cette baie damnée!*
[Let's get out of here.]

FRENCHIE 3: *Ramons!*
[Row!]

(*without standing up, the* FRENCHIES *row their way off stage stage right*)

URSULA: There they go, ladies! Let's sing them out of the bay. Good riddance to French rubbish.

ALL + AUDIENCE: Unite and unite, and let us all unite
For summer is acome unto day;
And whither we are going, we will all unite
In the merry morning of May!

WIFE 1: We always knew you were magic, Ursula Birdhood.

WIFE 2: Who needs menfolk? We can take care of ourselves!

WIFE 3: We have the Oss to look after us.

WIFE 4: O-oh. You shouldn't have said that, Betty.

WIFE 5: He's got that look in his eye!

WIFE 1: Now, Oss . . . We're respectable married women . . .

(*They back away from the* OSS)

ALL WIVES: Run!

(*Exit screaming and laughing, while the* OSS *chases them, lifting its skirts to try and cover them. Only* URSULA *is left*)

URSULA: There goes a beast with May in his blood. And there go the Frenchies, devil take them. God send back our menfolk in as much of a hurry. And then we'll dance in the Maytime all over again.

(*Exit, flicking her petticoats and skipping*)

# 'Hang on the Bell, Nelly!'

## 1460

## *Programme note*

During the War of the Roses, when the country was riven by civil war, a young Lancastrian tried to visit his sweetheart in Yorkish Chertsey. He was caught and condemned to hang. Having friends at court, he pinned his hopes on royal pardon – but how could it possibly arrive from London in time?

## Cast

| | |
|---|---|
| JUDGE | at least 6 CROWD MEMBERS |
| NEVILLE AUDELEY | HANGMAN |
| NELLY HERIOT | SEXTON |
| 2 GUARDS | MESSENGER |

## Costumes

• a few interesting hats for the women
• reversible apron for Nelly, one side pristine, the other torn, bloodstained
• mask for hangman

## Props

• short length of rope
• noose on a pole (e.g. a window pole)
• bell-rope (could be painted on backdrop, or imaginary)
• ladder, orchard-type
• scroll with a wax seal
• black cloth bag (not plastic!) (thin or Audeley's voice won't be audible)

## Special Effects

• pre-recordings of outdoor sounds: gaol footsteps and rattling keys (optional); galloping horse coming to a halt, neighing; tolling of church bell

## Safety Note

It is very important that no kind of noose should be rigged which would support any weight. Nor should it be left intact after the production. The ladder must be footed securely at all times – even when no one is climbing or sitting on it – in case it falls over.

# 'HANG ON THE BELL, NELLY!'

*A ladder stands against the back wall, footed by two members of the* CROWD. *The* JUDGE *sits three-quarters up it to pass judgement. The court is crowded with people.* AUDELEY *stands stage left arms gripped by his* GUARDS. *His hands are tied.* NELLY *stands stage front right, detached from the other spectators. A bell-rope hangs down at rear stage left*

JUDGE: Neville Audeley, this is the sentence of this court: that you be taken from here, to a place of imprisonment and from thence to a place of execution. At the sounding of the curfew bell you shall be hanged by the neck until you are dead. And may God have mercy on your soul.

NELLY: No! No, no! He didn't do anything! He isn't a spy! He only came here to visit me! No, no, you can't hang him!

CROWD 1: Shame. He's hardly more than a boy.

CROWD 2: Do we hang men now for going courting?

CROWN 1: That's civil war, for you. It makes the law too hasty.

CROWD 2: He was in the wrong place at the wrong time.

CROWD 3: Good riddance. He's a Lancastrian, isn't he? Lancastrians should keep well clear of us Yorkists if they don't want to get hanged.

CROWD 1: Don't talk so foolish! He only came visiting young Nelly Heriot. They were sweethearts long before this damned war turned us each against the other.

(*The* GUARDS *hustle* AUDELEY *away, stopping beside*
NELLY *for the two to speak to each other*)

NELLY:  Neville! I can't bear it!

AUDELEY:  Peace, Nelly. Don't cry. It will be all right. I've
sent word to London – to the King. I've got friends at
court. They won't fail me. The King won't let me . . . Oh
Nelly! Don't cry. Please don't cry!

(*He is hustled away. The* CROWD *is dispersing. One
couple drifts past* NELLY, *still talking*)

CROWD 4:  Well, I say it's a wicked shame. Young boy like
that.

CROWD 5:  May not be so bad. They say he's sent to
London for a King's pardon.

CROWD 4:  Oh yes? And could you ride to London and
back before the ringing of the curfew bell? Can't be done,
I say. Not a chance! He'll hang and his reprieve will come
an hour after. Bet you.

(NELL *overhearing this, clasps her head in her hands and
turns to look at the bell-rope, then runs off stage crying.
The stage empties but for two people who take down
the ladder and hold it horizontally to represent the bars
of a prison cell.* AUDELEY *is placed behind it by his*
GUARDS. *He grasps the bars of the cell*)

AUDELEY:  All at once I wish Time would stand still – the
sun stop moving across the sky. But it doesn't. It won't.
I've never known it move so quickly. Like a cannonball
out of a gun. Big yellow cannonball. See the shadow fly
round the sundial. Sweeping my life away.

Oh Nelly! No, I mustn't think of her. She's better off
without me. A Yorkist and a Lancastrian; it would never
have worked. Listen. They've stopped hammering. All day
they've been hammering, building the gallows. I thought
it was the worst noise I'd ever heard. But it wasn't. The

worst noise is the silence now they've stopped. It means the gallows are finished.

Oh Nelly! Where are you? Perhaps if you were here, I could be brave! Couldn't you even have come and said goodbye?

(*Hollow ringing footsteps and rattle of keys. Enter* WARDER)

WARDER: It's time, Audeley.

AUDELEY: No! It can't be! It's early yet.

WARDER: Ten minutes off curfew, according to the sun-dial on St Peter's. I just saw the sexton going up there to ring the bell.

(*We too see the* SEXTON *walking the full width of the stage to stand beneath the bell-rope*)

AUDELEY: But my reprieve! What about my reprieve?

WARDER: If it comes after curfew, we'll paste it on your tombstone.

(*The* WARDER *leads* AUDELEY *off stage front left, down stage steps into hall, then up again. Meanwhile, the* GUARDS *holding the ladder move it back to its earlier position and* CROWD MEMBERS *enter with a table which they stand in front.* AUDELEY *climbs the ladder and stands on the table. The* HANGMAN *scrambles up beside him. Another* CROWD MEMBER *comes on holding a long pole with noose dangling from it, and stands alongside. The* SEXTON *looks towards the 'church clock'. The stage fills with spectators.* AUDELEY *studies their faces, looking for* NELLY. HANGMAN *pulls a black bag from his belt*)

HANGMAN: Still looking for a friendly face to cheer you, boy?

AUDELEY: My sweetheart, yes. I didn't want her to come. I don't want her to see . . . any of this. But the thought of never seeing her again . . . her face. I can't remember her face. If I could just see her . . . I might find more courage . . .

HANGMAN: There's not many manage to keep up a brave face, Master Audeley. Don't you worry.

(HANGMAN *puts the noose around his neck and goes to put the bag over* AUDELEY'S *head.* AUDELEY *pulls his head away*)

AUDELEY: What's the time? I can't see the church clock from here.

HANGMAN: Must be right on curfew, sir. All you have to do is listen for the first stroke of the bell. I'll make sure you don't hear the second. Trust me. I'm good at my job.

(*The* SEXTON *pushes up his shirtsleeves, reaches up and 'pulls' on the bell-rope. Small, dull thud. He tries again, obviously mystified. The* CROWD *all put one hand up to their ears. Fade in the noise of birdsong, traffic, laughter, footsteps, a dog barking while action on the stage freezes but for the* SEXTON *pulling on the bell-rope. A long wait*)

CROWD 1: Sexton's late, isn't he?

CROWD 2: It must be time by now.

CROWD 3: Never known him be late, not in fifteen year.

CROWD 4: Maybe he's turned Lancastrian. (*Nervous laughter*)

CROWD 5: Should we go and see what's happened?

AUDELEY: Oh God! Can fear play such tricks on your mind? The seconds feel whole minutes long. Oh God, where's that cursed bell?

(*There is a further wait before galloping hooves off, neighing, clatter*)

MESSENGER: (*enters breathless, running*) Wait! Wait! Stop

the execution in the name of the King! A reprieve! I have a reprieve from the King!

(*General uproar.* MESSENGER *passes scroll up to the* HANGMAN *who reads it*)

AUDELEY: What's happening? In God's name, won't someone tell me what's happening?

HANGMAN: Looks like your reprieve came after all.

(*He removes noose and hood and unties* AUDELEY's *hands*)

Seems the King doesn't want you hanged today.

CROWD 1: Reckon God himself didn't want him hanged, or he'd have been dead before now. What happened to the curfew bell?

CROWD 2: Yeah! Why didn't it ring?

CROWD 3:  Was it a miracle, do you suppose?

CROWD 4:  Let's go and find out, eh?

*(They leave* AUDELEY *on the table, carrying off the ladder and taking a roundabout route to reach the* SEXTON, *who is still pulling his bell-rope)*

SEXTON:  Can't make it out, and that's the truth. I pull and pull, but not a sound comes out. It's just like the bell caught cold and lost its voice! If you set up that ladder, I'll go up and take a look.

*(They lean the ladder against the back wall utmost stage left, and foot it securely. The* SEXTON *climbs it, looking upwards as if at a bell. When speaking, he must turn his head and shoulders so as to be audible)*

Looks like there's something wrapped around the clapper of the bell. Something red and white.

*(Climbs to the top)*

There is! It's a . . . bless my soul. Would you believe it! In all my years, I've never seen the like! Well, blow me down! Fancy that! To think that I was pulling all that time, and all that time there was . . . well, bless my soul!

ALL:  Why didn't the bell ring?

SEXTON:  Because there was a girl inside it, that's why!

*(General consternation)*

She's there still. Sort of wrapped around the clapper, hanging on for dear life. It's little Nelly Heriot. Let go, child. Come down! Quick! Someone go up the stairs and get her down. She must have been beaten senseless by me swinging that bell . . . it's a wonder she's still alive.

*(Some exit stage left.* NELLY *is carried on from stage left by the* CROWD, *bloodstained and ragged)*

NELLY: No, no, I mustn't let go! I mustn't give up! The curfew mustn't ring. Not tonight! Not tonight!

CROWD 1: Hush now, child. All's well. All's well. The bell didn't ring.

CROWD 2: We didn't hang your young man.

CROWD 3: And now the message has come that you were waiting for.

(*The crowd makes way for* AUDELEY, *who has climbed down from the table and comes to her side*)

NELLY: Neville?

AUDELEY: Yes, it's me. I'm not a ghost. The King has spared my life. You and the King.

(*Enter the* JUDGE)

JUDGE: What's going on? What's going on? Why hasn't this man been hanged? You people shouldn't be here. No one should be on the streets after curfew. It's against the law. Sexton?

SEXTON: Begging your pardon, Your Honour, but curfew hasn't rung yet tonight.

JUDGE: Then get you up to the church this instant and ring it.

(*Instead of obeying, everyone looks at* NELLY *as if to ask permission*)

NELLY: Yes, Sexton. Now you may ring the bell.

ALL: Yes, Sexton. Now you may ring the bell.

(*Exit* SEXTON. *The tolling of a bell begins off stage. It provides the rhythm for the song, which begins with one voice and picks up one more with each line until the whole cast (and, with encouragement, the audience) are singing as they exit*)

AUDELEY AND OTHERS:  Hang on the bell, Nelly
Hang on the bell!
Your poor Neville's locked in a cold prison cell
As you swing to the left
And you swing to the right
Remember the curfew must never ring tonight.

(*Repeat*)

# A Murder Mystery

## 1483

## Programme note

No one will ever know for certain what became of the Princes in the Tower. This is the version Henry Tudor (who took Richard III's life and crown) would like us to believe.

## Cast

MOTHER

DAUGHTER

PRINCE EDWARD

PRINCE RICHARD

GAOLER

ACCOMPLICE/LOUT

## Costumes

- 2 mob caps
- 2 aprons
- 2 murderers' hoods/balaclavas
- velvet waistcoats and tights, perhaps, for princes
- gold headband for Prince Edward

## Props

- washline, dolly pegs and miniature items of washing
- bedroll with integral pillows and coverlet (see illustration)
- 2 pillows
- washbasket
- ball (optional)
- letter

## Idea!

This play is so slight that it could be performed front of curtain while a larger, more complex scene is prepared.

The children should also be encouraged to look at history as propaganda. Who might have killed the little princes, and why?

# A MURDER MYSTERY

*The stage represents the tower and the 'courtyard' action takes place on the floor in front of the stage. There is an imaginary window stage front centre. Two non-acting members of cast sit on the edge of the stage holding either end of a washline. On this will be hung various pieces of miniature washing and the murderers' hoods. Stage centre, a bedroll with pillows, on a sloping support, represents a double bed. The PRINCES perform entirely in mime. Only MOTHER, DAUGHTER and LOUT speak.*

(*Enter the PRINCES and obsequious GAOLER, who is showing them into their 'luxurious' rooms carrying their rolled up 'bed' as baggage.*

*Enter below MOTHER and DAUGHTER, the MOTHER with a basket of washing which she hangs up on a line. The PRINCES look round, uneasily, but quickly cheer up and explore, descending to lower area to play catch. DAUGHTER fetches the ball back and they let her join in. Then they return above, and wave to the DAUGHTER from the 'window' before returning to the 'bedroom'*)

DAUGHTER: Mother. Mother, who are the boys in the fine coats who came to the Tower today, with all those servants and all that fine baggage?

MOTHER: That's Prince Edward, my dear, and his brother Richard. Their father is newly dead of a fever. So soon young Prince Edward will be crowned. Think of it! Crowned King of England at twelve!

DAUGHTER: Poor souls.

MOTHER: (*laughing*) Why do you say that? The Tower of

London isn't all dungeons and guardrooms, you know. I hear the state apartments are very fine.

DAUGHTER: No, no. Poor boys to have lost their father, I mean.

(*Enter* GAOLER *above. No longer polite, he delivers a letter to* EDWARD, *who reads it and looks aghast.* LOUT *enters below and, cupping hands round mouth, shouts up at window*)

LOUT: Who's your father, my lord Bastard?

(*Enter* MOTHER *and* DAUGHTER *below. Together they collect the washing off the line into the basket again*)

DAUGHTER: Mother. Mother, when is Prince Edward going to be crowned? The coronation never seems to come. Today I heard a servant shout out and call the Prince . . . a rude name.

MOTHER: Ah, child. There'll be no coronation now. It's said that Edward was born illegitimate. He cannot be King. Their uncle is going to be crowned instead: King Richard III.

DAUGHTER: Poor boys.

MOTHER: Mmmm, but to be King at twelve and to carry the whole weight of government . . . That would have been a hard life for a boy.

DAUGHTER: No, no. Not to lose the crown. I meant poor boys to be called names by their own servants.

(*They exit with washing in basket. The* PRINCES *come and stand at the window, breathing on the imagined glass, wiping it clear with their sleeves. They look miserable, scared. Enter* DAUGHTER *and* MOTHER *with washing again, which they hang out*)

DAUGHTER: Mother. Mother, why do the Princes never play in the Tower gardens any more? I see them at the windows, looking out, and they look so sad and pale.

MOTHER: I think, child, that their palace is become a prison, and they're kept locked up tight, for fear the people rise up and call for Edward to be King rather than his uncle. The world is a wicked, politicking place these days.

DAUGHTER: Poor dears.

MOTHER: What, to be squabbled over like a pair of dice? Yes, I agree.

DAUGHTER: No, no. Not to be able to play out of doors, I mean.

*(They exit with the empty basket;* DAUGHTER *waves to the* PRINCES *but they do not wave back. They turn and go droopily back to the bed where they take off their jackets and lie down.*

*Enter* GAOLER *and* ACCOMPLICE. *They take hoods from the washline, climb to the stage and, with pillows, suffocate the* PRINCES, *who struggle, then fall still. Exit murderers*

*Enter* MOTHER *and* DAUGHTER *with empty washbasket and together they collect washing.* DAUGHTER *looks repeatedly up at the window)*

DAUGHTER: Mother. Mother, where are the Princes? I never see them at the window any more.

MOTHER: Shshsh, my dear. No more questions. Best to keep silent in these wicked times.

DAUGHTER: (*alarmed*) Tell me! I want to know! What's happened to Edward and Richard?

MOTHER: I'll tell you what people are saying . . . But you're not to go repeating it to a soul, do you hear me? They say that King Richard gave the orders for them to be killed. He told James Tyrrell to get it done – the most ambitious man at court. And Tyrrell summoned two men who would do the deed and keep silent after . . .

DAUGHTER: Oh Mother, no!

MOTHER: What could two little boys do against two grown men? I expect it was over quickly for them. People the likes of us are expected to forget those little princes ever lived, ever existed . . . and you, my girl, you'd best do just that.

DAUGHTER: (*incredulous, hysterical*) King Richard did that? But why? He already had the crown! He didn't need to! Why did he need to kill them? His own nephews!

MOTHER: (*restrains her bodily, hand over her mouth*) Hush, child. Speak lower. Perhaps he did. Perhaps he didn't. These are not the right times to question what we're told.

DAUGHTER: Poor souls!

MOTHER: Yes. I know. They were children. No older than you are, my love.

DAUGHTER: (*pulling away, dignified, bitter*) I didn't mean the Princes, Mother. I meant us. You and me. To live in a world that's run on lies and ambition, and have no voice to speak out against it.

(*She picks up the basket and carries it off stage.* MOTHER *pauses to consider these words, then follows*)

# 'Little Jack Horner
# sat in a Corner'
## 1537

## *Programme note*

Henry VIII's Dissolution of the Monasteries began as a much-needed reform. But it soon turned into the Great Pillage, with Henry and his friends grabbing vast areas of land and fortunes in Church treasure. John Horner, steward at Glastonbury Abbey, is reputed to have been sent on a last, fruitless mission to save the finest monastery of them all.

## Cast

JOHN HORNER
LANDLORD
at least 7 CUSTOMERS

## Costumes

- anything lower-class Tudor

## Props

- pie with removable pastry lid
- tightly rolled 'deed'
- tankards
- stools
- small table

## Idea!

Ask children to find out the history behind other nursery rhymes: e.g. 'London Bridge is Falling Down', 'Ring a Ring of Roses', 'Georgy Porgy', 'Pop Goes the Weasel'.

# 'LITTLE JACK HORNER SAT IN A CORNER'

*One small table and stool, to front and side of stage.* LANDLORD *stands drying beer tankard.* CUSTOMERS *sit about, their stools grouped as if round tables, chatting, playing cards.*

*(Enter* JACK *with pie. Sits down at table where he sets pie. Looks miserable.* LANDLORD *approaches.* JACK *picks pie up with guilty speed.* LANDLORD *gives him a funny look)*

JACK: A pint of ale, if you please, landlord. Mulled. It's a cold day.

LANDLORD: *(going to fetch ale)* And it could be a long cold winter, too. My master out of a living. Me out of a job. The roof gone from over my head.

*(*LANDLORD *brings pint.* JACK *has to move pie again)*

LANDLORD: *(pointedly)* You won't be wanting any of me wife's pie, then.

JACK: Pardon?

LANDLORD: We do sell pies here, you know. Generally speaking, customers don't feel a need to bring their own. I mean, you'll have people thinking my wife's cooking's not fit to eat.

JACK: Oh! The pie! No! No! This isn't mine. It's a present. I'm taking it from the Abbot of Glastonbury to the King. A token of goodwill. For Christmas!

LANDLORD: Ah. I get you. A bribe to make the King think

twice about dissolving the Abbey. Reckon it'll take more than a pie to keep the King's paws off Glastonbury!

JACK: (*to be rid of him*) A Christmas gift, that's all.

LANDLORD: Take more than a pie to sweeten the King's nature!

(*Moves off, laughing*)

JACK: (*to himself*) But then this is quite a pie. I was there when it was baked. I saw the 'meat' that went inside.

(*Picks pie up and shakes it*)

No gravy in here. (*To audience*) Do you know the recipe? Go on. Guess. You'll never guess. The deeds to twelve estates, that's what. It's a bribe, all right. My master the Abbot is giving the King twelve estates owned by the Abbey in the hope it'll be spared. Fields, woods, horses, pheasants, peasants, duckponds . . . There's a whole land-scape in this pie. Half a county almost.

CUSTOMER 1: I hear St Helen's has gone, then. Everyone turned out of doors – monks, servants, everyone! And the place stripped bare.

CUSTOMER 2: Like at Syon Park – St Briget's, you know? Nuns standing about like skittles in an alley. Nowhere to say their prayers or do their sewing.

CUSTOMER 3: (*sarcastic*) Ah, shame. St Briget *will* be put out.

CUSTOMER 2: Well, everyone else was, tee hee!

CUSTOMER 1: Out they went. Bags and baggage.

CUSTOMER 3: Bags and baggages, you mean.

JACK: (*still to himself, gloomily*) Those Royal Commissioners reported back that our Abbey was 'a house fit for the King's Majesty and no man else'. The Abbot will never keep King Henry at bay now. He's like a little boy picking over a tableful of sweets. Taking the best pickings for himself, then letting his friends join in.

CUSTOMER 4: In Lincolnshire the people rose up, object-ing.

CUSTOMER 5: Soon sat down again though, didn't they?

CUSTOMER 6: Down Exeter way I hear folk rushed to the church when they heard. Found some poor gump taking the place apart – threw stones at him. Chased him clear up the tower! Had to jump out of a window to get away!

CUSTOMER 7: Why'd they do that? Blowed if I'd put up a fight for those fat windbags up the priory. Would you? They live off our backs. They never do a hand's turn. And they forget their vows the moment they're tonsured.

CUSTOMER 6: Maybe their memory leaks away through

the top of their 'eads.

CUSTOMER 7: (*getting wildly carried away*) I'm all for the King 'bolishing the Church.

CUSTOMER 6: (*feeling they may have gone too far*) Well, not all of it, maybe.

CUSTOMER 7: No. Not all. And you and I won't be any the richer, that's for sure.

CUSTOMER 3: Oh, I don't know. I went up St Mary's after it was dissolved: got myself some lovely carved wood doors.

CUSTOMER 2: I hear there's pigs eating out of marble fonts in some parts.

JACK: (*still to himself*) And what about me? Nobody cares what will happen to me if Glastonbury is dissolved. I'm just the Abbey steward, me. A man could starve.

(*He pokes at the pie, nibbles a piece of crust*)

Dissolution they call it. How do you dissolve a monastery? Or a nunnery? Or a university? Salt you can dissolve, yes.

(*Absent-mindedly shakes some into his beer mug*)

Soda, yes. But great edifices half as high as the sky? Whole communities? What about the monuments? And the bones under them? Can you dissolve prayers? Or candleshine?

(*Pokes the pie again*)

This might work, of course . . . Nah. The King will just rub his hands and say, 'There's twelve, now let's have the rest!' Twelve estates! Gone to a man with more land than he could ever walk over.

(*Slams the table so that the pie jumps*)

Oo 'eck. The pastry's come adrift.

(*We see temptation take root. He takes a hasty sup of beer; it's salty and disgusting*)

Suppose the Abbot only put in eleven deeds. King would never know. If King takes the bribe, the estates are gone anyway. If he dissolves the Abbey, they're gone. I could just . . . He'd never know. He'd never know it was even in here.

(*Furtively, he filches one deed out of the pie; puts back the lid, then says in a rush:*)

If the Abbey's spared, I'll give it straight back to the Abbot! He'll thank me, won't he! . . . But which one is it? I daren't look.

CUSTOMER 1: The Great Pillage, they're calling it.

CUSTOMER 3: Lovely carved oak doors.

JACK: (*Peeps. Sits very upright. Squeaky noises of suppressed ecstasy*) It's Mells! Mells! The plum! The best of the bunch. Ahhaaagugg. Guggug. Mells! Holy Saint Everybody! It's Mells!

(*Gets up and dances round the stage, in and out of the tables, oblivious, then sits down again, bolt upright, grinning stupidly*)

LANDLORD: (*concerned*) You all right, sir?

JACK: Me? I'm fine.

(LANDLORD *makes to go*)

No! Don't go! Have a drink! In fact – give everybody a drink. On me. Drinks are on me.

LANDLORD: Very kind of you, sir, I'm sure. Who should I say is buying?

JACK: (*collects himself. Sits back grandly, practising a few posh poses*) 'A man of property', say. Jack Horner. John Horner of Mells in Somerset. Say, John Horner of Mells.

(*Beams round, acknowledging thanks with regal waves of his hand*)

CUSTOMERS:  Little Jack Horner sat in a corner.

LANDLORD:  Eating his Christmas pie.

ALL:  He put in his thumb and pulled out a plum and said:

JACK:  What a good boy am I, am I.

ALL:  And said:

JACK:  What a good boy am I!

# The Flanders Mare

## 1540

*Programme note*

Jane Seymour has died in childbirth. Henry VIII is without a queen. To remedy matters, he asks around for suitable candidates. But lacking the energy to go courting for himself, he commissions Hans Holbein to paint likenesses of the two most promising girls . . .

## Cast

HENRY VIII

THOMAS CROMWELL

4 COURTIERS

ANNE OF CLEVES

LADY-IN-WAITING

ARCHBISHOP CRANMER

other MEMBERS OF COURT, if desired

RECORDER PLAYERS

## Costumes

- large padded stomach, black armband and Tudor hat
- long opaque bridal veil to cover from head to foot
- teacher's robe and black Tudor hat for Cromwell
- bishop's mitre and stole
- various cloaks

## Props

- fresh, cooked chicken legs and bread
- 2 picture frames
- handkerchief
- bench

## Idea!

Anne's face should never be visible, so that her beauty (or lack of it) comes across purely from people's reactions to it.

# THE FLANDERS MARE

*The stage is bare except for a bench seat at centre back of stage.* HENRY *sits here, roast chicken leg in one hand, hunk of bread in the other, looking at two large, framed pictures held up by* COURTIERS 1 AND 2 *who have their backs to the audience, so that neither portrait can be seen.* CROMWELL *stands by, offering advice and looking smug.*

HENRY: *(talking through a mouthful of food)* Well? What do you think, Cromwell?

CROMWELL: *(obsequiously)* A difficult choice, Your Majesty.

HENRY: This Holbein fellow has done a fine job. A fine job . . . Just tell me again: which is which?

CROMWELL: The one on the left is Anne. The one on the right, Amelia.

HENRY: And they're Lutherans, eh?

*(He 'dips' between the portraits)*

Ip dip dox,
The cat's got the pox,
The dog got the Black Death and out goes . . .
You say the older one plays no music?

CROMWELL: But she is a very fine needlewoman, I understand.

HENRY: And there are more important things than music.

*(Dips again)*

Eeny meeny macker acker air eye domino
Eeny meeny macker acker om pom . . .

I'd rather acquaint myself with the lady face to face, you know?

CROMWELL: Naturally, Your Highness.

HENRY: Especially if I'm going to *marry* her.

CROMWELL: Perhaps Your Majesty is not ready yet to remarry. Perhaps the memory of the poor dear Queen is still too fresh in you?

HENRY: Mmmm. Poor little Jane. (*Pause, then briskly, with relish*) Still. Something must be done. I do so detest wearing black. If I have to choose, let it be . . .

(*He shuts his eyes, turns round and points, first at* CROMWELL, *turns again and points at left-hand portrait*)

. . . Amelia.

CROMWELL: That's Anne, Your Majesty.

HENRY: Anne, then. Fine face. Send ambassadors to Cleves to woo her, right away. And convey my compliments to Mr Holbein. The man has talent.

(*Exit* HENRY)

CROMWELL: (*aside*) Let's hope Mr Holbein has not 'improved' too much on the original.

(*Exit* ALL *with pictures*

*Enter* HENRY *with* COURTIERS 1, 2, 3 AND 4, *stage right, all in a row, wearing similar cloaks but entirely unlike him: girls, very small or very thin*)

HENRY: Come along, gentlemen! I can't wait. My fiancée's ship docks today and I mean to surprise her at Rochester. My royal person will never be noticed if we all travel together. I shall simply blend in.

(*Stands alongside them; pause for the absurdity of this to sink in*)

By the mass, I feel as nervous as the first time I married. Come, gentlemen! To Rochester! I must meet this woman who is to be my Queen!

(*Exit* HENRY *stage left*

HENRY *and* ANNE *enter from opposite sides of the stage,* HENRY's COURTIERS *behind him in a row.* ANNE's *face must never be seen. She is shrouded from head to foot in a wedding veil*)

HENRY: Oooo, here she is! Here she comes! My wife-to-be!

ANNE: (*startled*) My lord King! You do me too great an honour!

(*Curtseys very deeply*)

HENRY: Yes, yes. Never mind that. Get up. Get up, my dear, and let me look at you! My heart's afire already!

(*He lifts the veil*)

Ugh?

COURTIER I (aside): I think the fire just went out.

COURTIER 2: What a dog!

COURTIER 3: Shame about the smallpox scars.

COURTIER 4: Oh, I don't know. She's very homely.

COURTIER I: My mother-in-law is homely.

HENRY: Alas! Whom shall men trust? She looks like nothing so much as a great . . . *Flanders mare!* Where's Cromwell? Where's that daubing Holbein? I'll have their heads for this! Argch!

ANNE: Is that he? The man I am to marry? (Exit Anne stage right, rest stage left)

(*Enter* HENRY *without cloak, closely followed by*

*anxious* CROMWELL)

HENRY: Cancel the wedding!  Tell them I've changed my mind!

CROMWELL: But the betrothal is made, my lord!  The plans are all in hand!

HENRY: Then change them!  I won't be yoked to that . . . that . . . that *Flanders mare!*

CROMWELL: But to break off the marriage would insult all Lutherans beyond measure!  All Europe would side with Flanders against us.

HENRY: You should have thought of that before you saddled me with this horse-faced house-frau.  I hold you personally responsible for this, Cromwell.  Either extricate me or prepare to sell your hats.

CROMWELL: My hats, your Majesty?

HENRY: You won't be needing them once your head is off!

CROMWELL: We have looked in to the lady's background but her life has been blameless.  The Lady Anne is just very . . . she's very . . . Very . . .

HENRY: Ugly.  That's what she is.  Ugly ugly ugly.  Argch! Do I really deserve this?  A man of my . . .

COURTIER 1 (aside):  Girth?

COURTIER 2: Age?

COURTIER 3: Reputation?

COURTIER 4: Track record?

HENRY: Stature.  Do I deserve such a cruel fate?  I, a writer of love songs?  I, the acme of fashion?  I, a man of vigour and lusty gusto!

COURTIER 1 (aside): Lusy gusto?

COURTIER 2: Gusty bluster.

COURTIER 3: Gutsy muncher.

COURTIER 4: Dusty lust.

HENRY: (howls) Must I run my head into this yoke?

CROMWELL: (soothingly) Of course not, Your Majesty ...

HENRY: Aha!

CROMWELL: If Your Majesty is willing for a war with Europe.

(HENRY *gives exasperated roar and leaves stage left. Rest exit stage right*

*Enter* RECORDER PLAYER(S) *who strike up wedding march. Enter* HENRY *and* COURTIERS. HENRY *silences* RECORDER(S) *and has them play the funeral march. Enter* ANNE (*and* LADY-IN-WAITING) *heavily veiled.*

*Dumb-show wedding.* HENRY *looks around, bored. Spots a pretty face in the audience and winks, flirts, wiggles his fingers at her, ignoring* CRANMER)

CRANMER: I now pronounce you man and wife. You may kiss the bride.

HENRY: Urgch. You can kiss her if you like, but me, I'm going hunting.

(*Pauses on way out to have a word with* CROMWELL)

Get rid of her. Send her away somewhere. Richmond. Anywhere! (*Menacing*) For the sake of her health.

(*Blows a kiss to the girl in the audience then exits*)

CRANMER: Not an auspicious beginning to married life.

ANNE: What will happen now?

COURTIER 1: It will never last.

COURTIER 2: His eye is roving already.

COURTIER 3: But will it be divorce . . .

COURTIER 4: Or the Other Thing.

(*They all cup hands round their throats, including* ANNE)

ANNE: Now God spare me the fate of his second wife.

ALL: (*Mime taking off their heads and carrying them under one arm*) Anne Boleyn.

(CRANMER *leads the wedding procession off stage with solitary* ANNE *lagging behind*

*Enter* CROMWELL *and* ANNE, *she holding a handkerchief up to her face, he comforting, solicitous. They sit down on a bench at the back of the stage and mime a conversation. Enter* LADY-IN-WAITING, *harassed, long face, solemn voice*)

LADY-IN-WAITING: Cromwell is with her now, poor lady.

He says that if she agrees to a divorce, she will still be treated, in all respects, like a queen.

(*Puts one hand behind her ear, as if eavesdropping*)

He is offering her a pension of £4000 a year to live on. And a house or two. But will she accept? Will she agree to give up that most coveted title: Queen of England? Will she be willing to divorce the greatest husband in the land?

(ANNE *jumps to her feet, back to audience, thrusts both fists in the air and whoops*)

ANNE: Yes! Oh yes! Yes! Yes! Wonderful! Thank you! Thank you. Hallelujah! Thank God! Yes! A thousand times yes!

(*Collects herself and curtseys gravely, returning handkerchief to her face.* CROMWELL *bows. They exit sedately*)

LADY-IN-WAITING: Phew. That was close. She's accepted. All's well. King Henry VIII is free to marry again. A fifth wife. Even a sixth, why not? And the Flanders Mare is to go . . . (*looks for the right word*) out to grass . . .

(LADY-IN-WAITING *exits, pausing at stage edge to say:*)

Lucky girl!!!

# Walter Raleigh
# Salutes the Queen

## 1580

## *Programme note*

It is not known exactly how Walter Raleigh first
met Queen Elizabeth I. This is the traditional
explanation of how an obscure (if charming)
country gentleman rose within months to be
one of her court favourites.

## Cast

| | |
|---|---|
| WALTER RALEIGH | MAYOR |
| FITCHETT, his manservant | 2 FOPS |
| QUEEN ELIZABETH I | large CROWD OF PEASANTS |

## Costumes

I have treated this play as an exercise in mime. Unless you use it to teach Tudor costume, no authentic costume is needed other than:
• small, glittering crown
• cloak, the outside magnificent, the inside brown
• chain of office

## Props

• bed

The Incredibly Useful All-Purpose Bed – on to a rectangle of hessian is sewn a layer of sheeting and a pillow. To the foot of this bed is attached a pseudo coverlet and turned down sheet. Cord-loop handles on each corner allow the bed to be folded in half with all the bedding on the inside (so that it looks like a bulky hessian bag). In use (ideally) the bed is used in conjunction with a wedge-shaped slope of solid construction, so that the pillow end is raised, and the actor's face can still be seen clearly by the audience. The cord loops at the top are used to 'hook' it onto the slope. (This slope is also useful for making the pond visible to the audience in *The Moonrakers*).

## Idea!

'Putting on clothes' is an excellent subject for mime, as it makes children aware of the precise elements involved in familiar movements.

Discuss whether boys or girls are the most vain about their appearance, and care most about clothes – and whether this was so in earlier times.

# WALTER RALEIGH
# SALUTES THE QUEEN

*The bed comes into play, supported on a ramp.* RALEIGH
*lies on it, curled up, asleep. The stage is otherwise empty.*

(RALEIGH *gradually wakes. Suddenly sits up*)

RALEIGH: Fitchett! Fitchett! Where are you?

(*Enter manservant with butler-like dignity*)

FITCHETT: Good morning, sir.

RALEIGH: It's today!

FITCHETT: Indeed it is, sir. No doubt about it. All day.
Until tomorrow.

RALEIGH: The Queen's visit, I mean! I'm going to meet
the Queen today!

FITCHETT: An honour which redounds on us all, sir.

RALEIGH: What's the weather doing?

FITCHETT: Raining, sir.

RALEIGH: Raining? That's bad. That's not good.

FITCHETT: Good for the peas, sir.

RALEIGH: Idiot. Rain's serious. In London it doesn't
matter, but out here – in the Awful Beyond – rain tips the
balance. Her Majesty won't like rain.

FITCHETT: She has no great tenderness for peas, you
think, sir?

RALEIGH: Quiet, Fitchett, and help me dress. Fetch me a
new shirt.

FITCHETT: A new shirt, sir? The one you slept in is not above three days old.

RALEIGH: Yes, but I won't wear the one I slept in, Fitchett. Fetch the one with the large ruff.

(*They mime the fetching and putting on of each successive garment*)

Now the doublet.

FITCHETT: Which doublet, sir?

RALEIGH: The bombast brocade. Now the short hose – the bronze ones with the slashes of orange. Now lace me together, Fitchett. And now the silver stockings.

FITCHETT: Which garters, sir?

RALEIGH: The ones with the gold tassels. No! Silver. Let's not be pretentious. The calfskin shoes. Can you do bows, Fitchett? Dashed if I can tie a good bow.

FITCHETT: Naturally, sir.

RALEIGH: The hat. And finally – the *cloak*.

FITCHETT: No breakfast this morning, sir?

RALEIGH: I'm too excited, Fitchett. I couldn't eat a thing. The cloak – and don't let it snag on the lid of the press!

FITCHETT: (*confiding to audience*) A cloak worth waiting for. Velvet: piped, interlined, gilt-clasped, silver-corded.

(*Fetches real cloak*)

Magnificent. A feast of a cloak. A pageant of a cloak.

RALEIGH: A man must dress in keeping with his social station.

FITCHETT: (*aside*) Or the one he's aiming at.

RALEIGH: Curse the rain. It will mar my velvet.

(*Exit left as* CROWD *rush in from right as if running ahead of a coach*)

BOY: She's coming! Girl, look at the livery!

WOMAN: I caught a glimpse of red hair.

MAN: I saw a hand waving!

ALL: It's stopping! The coach is stopping!

GIRL: Urgh, look. I trod in a puddle.

(*Lifts skirts and picks her way out; a deep puddle, obviously.* MAYOR *and* FOPS *sweep in from left, looking nervous but grand and puffed up.* RALEIGH *is in background, clearly not of great importance*)

BOY: She's getting down! Queen Bess is down! I see'd the Queen, Mam!

(*Everyone gasps as* ELIZABETH *enters. Token small diamanté crown but no attempt at replicating costume*)

GIRL: She looks like a fairy!

(*Following comments are shared between as many actors as make up the* CROWD)

CROWD: Those velvets and satins! That ruff of Spanish lace! Those gilt cords lacing her together! Those gems in her hair! Those pearls round her neck! All that embroidery! And petticoats. And fur trimmings!

RALEIGH: Those white cheeks!

BOY: She looks like a queen!

GIRL: She *is* a queen, booby.

(MAYOR *and everybody bow low.* MAYOR *stays bowed*)

MAYOR: (*rustic: patently a learned speech*) Welcome, Your beloved Majesty, to our little town – a town which holds you as dear in its affections as all your great Londons put together!

ELIZABETH: How kind.

MAYOR: Won't you pray enter my humble hall, Your Majesty and take a little refreshment after your long and tedious journey?

(ELIZABETH *starts across stage, but meets 'the puddle'. ALL gasp again, this time in horror*)

FOP 1: A puddle!

WOMAN: A gert brown, oozing sink of a puddle.

FOP 2: And those shoes are doe-skin or I'm a Dutchman.

(ELIZABETH *hesitates, moves to go round but cannot. Looks annoyed.* RALEIGH *steps forward, unfastening his cloak. Flourishes it with ridiculous panache . . .*)

FITCHETT: (*aside*) Oh, not the cloak. Please not the cloak!

(*. . . Then lays it over the puddle. The* CROWD *stare at the cloak in horror.* ELIZABETH *steps on to it and looks* RALEIGH *over, impressed*)

ELIZABETH: Does it always rain so much in these parts?

RALEIGH: Rain, Your Majesty? I thought the sun had been shining on me with all its brightness – ever since you stepped down from your coach.

(*The* CROWD *exchange glances. The* FOPS *look peeved, outdone. The* MAYOR *continues to look nervous.*

ELIZABETH *decides to be delighted*)

ELIZABETH: Your name?

RALEIGH: Raleigh, Your Majesty. Walter Raleigh in your everlasting thrall.

ELIZABETH: Your cloak is spoiled, Master Raleigh.

RALEIGH: It died in a worthy cause. Would that I might lie so low, if I could die so happily.

(ELIZABETH *even more pleased. They look at one another for some time. Then she crosses as far as the* MAYOR, *who*

*kisses her hand*)

ELIZABETH:  Does Master Raleigh dine with us today?

MAYOR: (*taken by surprise*) What, young Walter? Yes, he's invited – unless Your Majesty don't want him?

ELIZABETH: (*looking back at Raleigh*) Yes, yes! Let his chair be set close to mine. I like a man with . . . (*searches for the right word*) panache.

(*Exit* ELIZABETH *and all gentry but* RALEIGH *and two* FOPS. *As* CROWD *looks on,* FITCHETT *peels cloak up off floor with obvious grief*)

FITCHETT: There's no saving it, sir. The mud is right through to the lining!

RALEIGH:  It was worth the price.

FOP I: (*pained to* FOP 2) That cloak must've cost Walter ten guineas.

FOP 2: (*jealous*) Would that I had thought of investing a cloak so wisely.

FOP 1: Why? What d'you mean?

FOP 2: I mean Walter Raleigh is poorer by a cloak, and richer by a queen's good opinion. He's a made man, I tell you. A made man. Are you coming, Raleigh?

(*Sucking up. Drawing him off stage with an arm round his shoulders*)

Might I just ask where you buy your doublets? Always so tasteful. Always so stylish. I was just saying to Carmichael here . . .

FITCHETT: (*bitterly complaining*) Some people just can't be bothered to look after their belongings. I mean, I suppose I'm meant to try and resurrect this sodden object – rescue what I can, redeem the trimmings. Throw the rest away.

(CROWD *drift off right. As last woman goes, she calls back to him*)

WOMAN: What you wanna do is hang it up till the mud dries, give it a good shake, then brush it with good stiff brushes. Get the worst off, that will.

FITCHETT: (*waves a half-hearted acknowledgement*) He'll have to have a new one made, no question.

(*Suddenly sees his chance to own the splendid cast-off. Holds it against himself, inside out, swings it round him, swaggers up and down, bows, lays the cloak down with a flourish. Then puts it on and leaves, saying:*)

A feast of a cloak. A pageant of a cloak. What did she say? Hang it up. Let the mud dry. Give it a good shake. Brush with stiff brushes . . . It'll come up as good as new! A man could build a future on a cloak like this.

# Chicken and Bacon

## 1646

*Programme note*

Even in old age, Francis Bacon continued to apply his towering intellect to science. He believed that no scientific theory was valid until proven by empirical experiment. One snowy, bitter day, he set about proving the benefits of refrigeration . . .

## Cast

HORSE/NARRATOR
FRANCIS BACON (requires a certain gift for slapstick)
DR WITHERBORNE
EARL OF ARUNDEL
PEASANT WOMAN/MAID

## Costumes

- 2 long woolly scarves for Bacon and Witherborne
- apron
- reins and browband for horse
- 2 mourning top hats

## Props

- table
- bowl or basket
- large feathery chicken with opening for hand/stuffing
- bucket full of polystyrene 'snow'
- rubber, joke chicken
- serving platter
- bed (as before, p. 116)
- black plume
- spare polystyrene snow
- 4 forks (optional)

## Special Effects

- the chicken is, of course, animated by Bacon
- chicken noises can be supplied from off stage
- pre-recorded versions needed of the end 'chicken' music

## Idea!

This is a good 'first-half finisher'. It leaves the audience in a good mood, and the mess made by the polystyrene can be swept up in the interval.

# CHICKEN AND BACON

*On the left of the stage a table represents the carriage, and the* NARRATOR *represents the* HORSE *pulling it. She stands in front of the table, reins looped behind her neck and under her arms, a browband round her head.* BACON *and* WITHERBORNE *kneel up on the table, each an arm round the other, swaying and jogging with the 'motion'. Stage right,* PEASANT WOMAN *feeds invisible chickens from a bowl*

HORSE: It was March and very cold. Snow too bright for your eyes. Ice underfoot. Cobwebs like chain mail in the hedges. Bitter, bitter cold.

BACON: . . . But consider how such processes ruin the taste of food! Meat too tough. Fish too salt. And pickling! Well, pickling's only fit for gherkins!

WITHERBORNE: I have observed, in the past, that the cooler the pantry, the fresher the food.

HORSE: That's Dr Witherborne, the King's physician.

BACON: Hmmm. Heat certainly quickens the rate of decay. Ergo: the lack of heat should very probably . . .

HORSE: And that's Francis Bacon: lawyer, poet, scientist, politician and general, all-round genius. One-time Lord Chancellor to King James.

BACON: (*point towards the 'house'*) Hmmm. Now supposing I took one of those chickens . . . Stop! Stop the carriage!

HORSE: (*rearing to a halt*) Watch it! I'm valuable horse flesh, me! It wouldn't take much to have me over, in all this snow.

(BACON *jumps down and runs to 'house', bangs on invisible door*)

WITHERBORNE:  Where are you going, Bacon?

WOMAN:  Good afternoon, sir.

BACON:  I want to buy a chicken.

WOMAN:  Oh well, them in the yard is my layers, sir. I don't really keep them to sell. Oi!

(BACON *pushes past her*)

BACON:  I *must* have a chicken, madam! Science demands it. Theory is not enough. We must experiment in order to prove!

(*Rushes off stage right, saying:*)

And snow! Plenty of snow!

(WOMAN *looks at* WITHERBORNE *who shrugs helplessly.
She gives him a bucket, which he eyes as if he's never
seen one before, then hurries off to fill it, stage left.*
BACON *re-enters stage right holding a glove-puppet
chicken still 'alive'*)

HORSE:  Francis Bacon, well-known genius.

(*Lots of 'business' with the chicken which pitches him all
over the stage and maybe into the audience. Re-enter*
WITHERBORNE *with bucket of 'snow'.* BACON *sits down on
chair with chicken still struggling in his lap*)

BACON:  Now. If I cram the body cavity with snow . . .

HORSE:  Of course it might have been easier to have killed
the chicken first.

(*Lots more business with chicken,* BACON *wrestling it in
and out of the audience, periodically returning to chair
to go on 'stuffing'.*)

HORSE:  But at last it was done

BACON:  There!

　　　(*Pause while all three stare at the inert chicken*)

Bless me, Witherborne, suddenly I don't feel very well.

HORSE:  Neither does the chicken, by this time.

WITHERBORNE:  Bacon? My word, you do look a shade
pasty.

WOMAN:  It's all that snow against his stomach. Look, his
coat's wet through.

BACON:  I think I might just . . . lie down.

(*He keels over and the other two catch him and stand
him up again. This is repeated three or four times during
the following speeches*)

WITHERBORNE:  Let's get you back to the carriage, friend.

BACON: But what about the chicken?

WOMAN: Yes, what about my chicken?

WITHERBORNE: Here's a sovereign for your chicken, madam.

BACON: Don't lose sight of the chicken, whatever you do!

WOMAN: For a sovereign, you can have the bucket, too!

BACON: It won't rot, I tell you, Witherborne! It won't rot! My reputation on it! You just see if I'm not right!

WITHERBORNE: Very good, Francis, but let's get you home in the warm. A man could catch his death on a day like this.

(*They get back aboard the carriage,* BACON *moaning and clutching his stomach,* WITHERBORNE *holding the chicken in the bucket*)

HORSE: But Sir Francis was too ill to be driven all the way home. So they stopped at the house of a friend, the Earl of Arundel, just down the road.

(*Mime the following events: stage right is now* ARUNDEL's *house. He comes to the 'door'. The bed is brought on, and* BACON *'lies down' on it*)

The Earl was kindness itself. But he had not been expecting visitors. The beds were not aired. The sheets were damp.

BACON: Don't lose sight of the chicken, Witherborne!

HORSE: By morning, Bacon had pneumonia. Within days, he was dying.

BACON: (*frail, urgent, coughing*) Tell me quickly! How goes it with the chicken?

WITHERBORNE: The chicken is not decayed a jot. Not one jot. I believe you may have struck on something, Bacon, my dear old friend . . . Bacon? Bacon?

HORSE: (*sticks black plume into browband*) The great man was dead . . .

(*The death march plays, but abruptly stops*)

But he died happy. His theories about refrigeration had been proved right by empirical scientific experimentation. And a week later, they were still able to cook and eat the chicken . . .

(WITHERBORNE *and* ARUNDEL *put on top hats with long black crepe scarves round them. Enter* WOMAN *bearing rubber chicken on a platter and they all sit down to eat, including the horse*)

Well? People need a bite to eat after a funeral.

(*Fade in the 'chicken-tonight' theme or some such jolly music*)

# The Moonrakers

## 1650s

## Programme note

Dutch immigrants brought prosperity to the
Wiltshire wool industry, but missed their
favourite Holland gin, which import duty put
beyond reach. The local people came to their
aid, establishing an efficient smuggling network
for life's little luxuries – despite the Revenue
men. This play shows the origins of the term
'Moonraker' and why Wiltshiremen wear it
with such pride.

## Cast

TOM
DICK
HARRY
} Smugglers

CHORUS of at least 7, doubling as Revenue men

## Costumes

- black clothing for the chorus
- tricorn hats for 2 or 3 of the Revenue men
- rustic clothes for smugglers

## Props

- pond (does not need to be of a realistic size)
- rakes
- duck decoy quacker (or audience member can be told to quack)
- boot
- 7 electric torches
- pistols for 1 or 2 of the Revenue men
- keg

## Special Effects

- ideally the pond is made of some highly reflective substance (e.g. mylar) which will throw light up into the faces of the smugglers. If it is supported on a slope it will be more visible to the audience and the keg can be concealed beneath it.

## Idea!

If you have not got good black-out conditions, don't bother with the torches. Get the children to think of ways of implying blackest night.

# THE MOONRAKERS

*A centre aisle is needed, and rear access for the actors. This scene ideally calls for full black-out, with one spotlight. The set is black, with a glow-in-the-dark moon high up on the back curtain. A pond, stage centre.* CHORUS/REVENUE MEN, *dressed in black, carry (electric) torches*

(CHORUS *begin with their backs to the audience, each shining his torch upwards under his chin to illuminate face only. One after another, each turns to face audience and speak one line, so as to appear, one by one, as eerie faces*)

CHORUS 1:  Better a night when the moon is young
   And the stars have shut their eyes;

CHORUS 2:  A night when guard dogs bite their tongues
   And the shadows blindfold spies.

CHORUS 3:  Better a night when the moon is old
   And goes wrapped in rags of cloud;

CHORUS 4:  A night when the dark is biting cold
   And the rattling wind is loud.

CHORUS 5:  But if business calls when the moon is full,
   Better go out with four.

CHORUS 1:  With one to push

CHORUS 3:  And one to pull

CHORUS 4 AND 5:  And two to watch out for the Law.

(*They exit while shining their torches into the faces of the audience. Off: owl hoot, birdcall, decoy duck*)

TOM: All clear!

(TOM, DICK *and* HARRY *enter and converge on the pond, looking shady and secretive*)

DICK: What is it tonight, Tom? Brandy or rum?

TOM: A keg of best Holland gin, Dick. Bound for the woollenmen of Swindon. Last night it slept in a haystack south of Devizes. Tonight it'll fetch up where it belongs, at a price honest men can afford.

HARRY: Duty-free, you mean.

TOM: Duty? Don't talk to me about duty. Reckon it's the duty of every good Englishman to keep good liquor flowing through the English countryside – despite the Revenue men.

ALL: Revenue men!

(*They spit delicately*)

HARRY: So where are the goods hidden, then?

TOM: In the pond, Miller said. In the village pond.

DICK: Big pond. In the middle or at the edge?

TOM: Didn't say.

HARRY: You and I can feel about for it, with our rakes.

DICK: Can't I help? One of those kegs is right heavy.

TOM: You have to keep watch. Someone has to keep watch.

DICK: (*Looks around. Chooses someone in the audience (e.g. head teacher). Gives them duck decoy to blow*) You'll keep watch, won't you? It's easy. You just give a blow on this if you spy Revenue men a-creeping up on us, right?

(*They feel about in the pond with rakes*)

Anything your side, Tom?

TOM: Nothing. Anything your side, Harry?

HARRY: Not yet. Anything your side, Dick?

(*Enter* REVENUE MEN *creeping up the centre aisle, looking this way and that, turning round, walking backwards, fingers to their lips, shining their torches up into their faces. The* SMUGGLERS *ignore the duck quack which, it is hoped, grows more and more agitated*)

Ah, here's something!

(*Fishes boot out from under pond and slings it off stage*)

Nope. Must be deeper in.

DICK: Those ducks are kicking up a proper rumpus tonight.

TOM: Wake up the whole village carrying on like that.

(DICK *splashes* HARRY)

HARRY: Watch out! You're splashing me all over . . . Thought you were supposed to be keeping watch, Dick.

DICK: Oh, it's all right. I left one of them with the . . . oops!

(REVENUE MEN *climb on to stage*)

CAPTAIN: Aha! So what have we here? Halt or I fire.

(SMUGGLERS *freeze*)

A little late for weeding the pond, isn't it, gentlemen? Could it be that we have disturbed a nest of *smugglers*?

TOM: Ah!

HARRY: Ah!

DICK: Ah! Well now . . .

CAPTAIN: What's in the pond? Contraband gin? French wine? Belgian lace? Jamaican tobacco?

TOM: (*yokelish*) Now what you a-blathering about, man? This here's a village pond, not a village shop. No, look. The *moon* has dropped into our pond – see for yourselves. Walking home from the inn, we wuz, and Dick chanced to see it. The *moon*! In our pond! Think of that. How often does that happen, do you suppose?

DICK: Once in a blue *moon*, I'd say.

HARRY: We wuz just raking her out. Solid silver, maybe. What do you think?

DICK: Unless it's true she's made of cheese. I like a bite of cheese.

TOM: Care to help, gentlemen?

(*Holds out his rake to the Revenue* CAPTAIN *who reflexly takes it, then shoves it back in disgust*)

CAPTAIN: What a ninny!

2ND IN COMMAND: What noodles! What yokels! Drunk, I dare say, sir.

CAPTAIN: Not at all! They are all *moon*-touched, ha ha! All *lun*atics, ha ha! Moon fallen in the pond, indeed! Come, men, we've wasted enough time. There are smugglers abroad tonight, and I mean to feel their collars before morning!

(*They start to leave but the 5th can't resist looking for himself.* TOM *points out the moon in the pond and 5th looks amazed. Then the 4th comes back to fetch 5th away*)

REVENUE 4: It's a *reflection*, you noddle.

(*Exit* REVENUE MEN *laughing at stupidity of the yokels*)

REVENUE MEN: (*variously as they leave*) What idiots! Fools! Moon fallen in the pond, pah! Lunatics.

DICK: Phew. That was a close one.

TOM: Too close for comfort.

(TOM *and* HARRY *look resentfully at* DICK, *who in turn looks resentfully at the person in audience*)

DICK: Why didn't you signal?

TOM: Well, men, let's finish what we started.

(*They rake for the keg and drag it ashore with satisfied grunts*)

DICK: Five gallons of best Hollander gin.

TOM: Duty-free.

HARRY: I'll drink to that.

(*They go to exit,* DICK *remonstrating with the person in the audience for not warning them, and retrieving the duck decoy. He is last to leave*)

DICK: (*hesitates and speaks to audience*) Not a word now, you hear? Traps shut. Beaks buttoned. And watch the wall, my darlings, while the gentlemen go by.

(DICK *waves and exits.* CHORUS *repeat opening*)

CHORUS 1: Better a night when the moon is young
  And the stars have shut their eyes;

CHORUS 2: A night when guard dogs bite their tongues
  And the shadows blindfold spies.

CHORUS 3: Better a night when the moon is old
  And goes wrapped in rags of cloud;

CHORUS 4: A night when the dark is biting cold
  And the rattling wind is loud.

CHORUS 5: But if business calls when the moon is full,
  Better go out with four.

CHORUS 1: With one to push

CHORUS 3: And one to pull.

CHORUS 4 AND 5: And two to watch out for the Law!.

# The Village that Chose to Die

## 1665

## *Programme note*

In September 1665 a parcel of cloth was delivered to a tailor in the Peak District village of Eyam. In it was a cloud of fleas all the way from plague-stricken London.

## Cast

GEORGE VICCARS, a tailor
GOODWIFE VICCARS
their DAUGHTER
4 VILLAGERS – more, if desired
WILLIAM MOMPESSON, a priest
OUTSIDER
WIDOW

## Costumes

- long aprons for Goodwife and daughter
- black clothes for widow (optional)
- clerical collar and bib for Mompesson
- Puritan-type bonnets for women (optional)

## Props

- chair
- bolt of lightweight, fluid black cloth + an extra metre
- white tablecloth with confetti folded inside
- pulpit whose face will take chalk
- trowel for widow
- piece of chalk
- large Bible on lectern or small one to hold
- small bowl
- loaf

## Idea!

Suggest that three unknown members of class have the plague. Brushing against them, their belongings, chairs, etc., will bring infection and death. How do the class a) move b) feel? How many people do they think will be accidentally infected? At the end of the day, ask how they would react to Mompesson's request.

# THE VILLAGE THAT CHOSE TO DIE

*A pulpit stands upstage centre – a table up-ended would do, with low steps behind for the priest to mount. Downstage, right of centre, stands a table with a folded white cloth on it charged with confetti, and a chair to the right of it. There is no one on stage, except for* MOMPESSON, *hidden behind the pulpit*

*(Enter* GEORGE VICCARS *through audience, carrying a bolt of lightweight black cloth which he shows to members of audience, inviting them to touch, feel the weft, admire the quality. Once or twice he scratches. Jolly mood)*

GEORGE: See? It's just come. I've been waiting weeks for this! Enough to make five pairs of breeches – or two Sunday dresses.

*(He mounts the stage, unrolling some cloth to measure it against his arm)*

Come and see, goodwife! The cloth I ordered from London has come!

*(Enter* DAUGHTER*)*

DAUGHTER: I wish I could go to London, Papa. All those palaces and shops and people.

*(Enter* GOODWIFE, *tying her apron)*

GOODWIFE: Oh, no, you don't, child. It's a fearful place just now. They have the plague in among them like the devil himself. Hundreds dying every week. God pity the poor souls.

(*She slaps the back of one hand with the other*)

GEORGE: Well, wife? What do you think of my purchase?

GOODWIFE: (*not unduly upset*) I think your fine London cloth has brought fleas into my nice clean house, that's what I think. You and your cloth.

(*She takes one end of the cloth and holds it across her body, as if to see how a dress would look. The* DAUGH-TER, *too, steps up against the cloth and puts her arms over it.*

*Enter* VILLAGERS 1–4, *each in turn stepping up into the cloth, drawing it out across the stage till bolt-roll is empty.* GEORGE *sits down on the chair looking groggy, pulling at his collar, gradually feeling worse, resting his head on the table during the following. Pace slows*)

DAUGHTER: Your cloth.

VILLAGER 1: Your London cloth.

VILLAGER 2: Full of London fleas.

VILLAGER 3: Fleas full of London blood.

VILLAGER 4: Blood full of death.

ALL: The Black Death.

MOMPESSON: (*bobbing up from behind pulpit*) The plague.

GOODWIFE: Where shall we go to escape it?

DAUGHTER: To Auntie Mariah? Or cousin John?

VILLAGER 1: Not to London, that's for certain.

VILLAGER 2: Must get away, though.

VILLAGER 3: Must get the children away!

VILLAGER 4: Somewhere free of the plague!

MOMPESSON:  The plague . . .

(*They all turn towards him and kneel, a church congregation now, crossing themselves, still strung together with the black cloth*)

It travels about the country in the blood of those fleeing it. In trying to get away, folk carry a death sentence to another community of souls, condemning them, too, to die. When a fire breaks out, we protect the houses round about by making a firebreak, don't we? Starving the fire of new fuel. That's what we must do here.

(*One by one, in speaking, the congregation turn back to face the audience*)

GOODWIFE:  What is he saying?

VILLAGER 1:  What is he suggesting?

VILLAGER 2:  Not leave the village?

VILLAGER 3:  Not leave Eyam?

MOMPESSON:  As we are Christians, we must be prepared to die, in order that others may live.

GOODWIFE:  He made it sound so simple.

VILLAGER 1:  Isolate the disease so that the disease could die out.

VILLAGER 2:  Let the plague burn itself out. Here.

VILLAGER 3:  Here in Eyam.

ALL:  Here. Among us.

MOMPESSON:  Three hundred and fifty souls awaiting a terrible death. Men, women and children. Because I asked it of them. (*Reads from Bible*) 'Greater love hath no man than this: that a man lay down his life for his friends.' (*Looking up to heaven*) Into thy hands I delivered them, O Lord, to be a living sacrifice.

(GEORGE *rolls from his chair and lies dead on the floor. The congregation cover him with the black cloth.* MOMPESSON *descends from the pulpit. Quickening of pace. A feeling of urgency.* VILLAGERS *walk smartly across the stage 'showing' the things they are talking about. A remnant of the black cloth is held between* VILLAGER 3 *and* VILLAGER 4. *Their foreheads and cheeks are daubed with chalk*)

MOMPESSON: We didn't just give in to it. I locked up the church. It was a breeding ground for disease. I held my sermons in the open air instead, amid the smoke from fumigation fires, the summer heat.

VILLAGER 1: We did everything we could to protect ourselves – smoked clay pipes all day long.

VILLAGER 2: Wore charms and bunches of herbs round our necks.

VILLAGER 3: Carried nosegays to keep off the stench.

VILLAGER 4: As one person in the house fell ill, we chalked a cross on the door to warn the neighbours.

(*Chalks on front of pulpit*)

VILLAGER 1: We buried the bodies in lime.

VILLAGER 2: We buried them in our gardens, rather than carry them through the streets to the churchyard.

VILLAGER 4: We set up patrols to stop cowards . . . the less courageous trying to leave the village.

(VILLAGER 1 *makes a dash from stage left to stage right but is caught in the black strip of cloth held by* VILLAGER 3 *and* VILLAGER 4. *Mimed struggle then action freezes while* WIDOW *speaks. Pause. Slowing of pace*)

WIDOW: (*holding trowel*) I buried my husband, my three sons and three daughters in the field beside my house. Who will be left to bury me, I wonder?

(MOMPESSON *comes and puts a comforting arm round her. She weeps against his chest*)

MOMPESSON: In my heart of hearts, did I think God would spare us, if we showed willing? Like Abraham offering up Isaac, because God had asked it of him? If I did, I was wrong. Did I want to lead my whole parish to heaven in a single flock? Maybe. I can't remember now. Too ill to remember now.

(WIDOW *comforts him*)

VILLAGER 3: And if ever anyone came near the village . . .

(OUTSIDER *approaches from rear of the hall*)

OUTSIDER: . . . some tinker or traveller . . .

VILLAGER 3: . . . our sentries kept them away: *Stop!* Go back!

OUTSIDER:  Why? I'm on my way to Baslow. My way lies through Eyam.

VILLAGER 3:  Go back! Go round! We have the plague in Eyam. Go round us . . . and remember us in your prayers!

(OUTSIDER *stays put*)

VILLAGER 4:  (*with small bowl*) We needed supplies from outside, of course. We put the money for them in bowls of bleach, on the outskirts of the village.

(OUTSIDER *puts a loaf of bread on the edge of the stage, picks up the bowl and retires. Stage gradually empties*)

DAUGHTER:  Three-quarters of the villagers died. But Eyam didn't.

OUTSIDER:  Some other villages disappeared completely, abandoned by the dying, abandoned by the living. Nothing left. Not a trace.

DAUGHTER:  But Eyam survived. The Angel of Death passed over – eventually. Morning came after the long, dark night.

(*She picks up the folded white cloth and shakes it. Confetti flies up, as the fleas supposedly did from the black cloth. She leaves stage carrying the cloth*)

# Glencoe

## 1692

## Programme note

The MacDonald clan – so long a thorn in the side of King William III – has finally sworn the Oath of Allegiance. Peace can return to the bitter, winter glens. Indeed, the MacDonalds are even ready to offer hospitality and shelter to a loyalist Campbell regiment when it arrives in the glen. After all, they no longer have anything to fear from their former foes. Do they?

## Cast

| | |
|---|---|
| FATHER | GRANDFATHER |
| MOTHER | GRANDMOTHER |
| BROTHER | ANGUS, a Campbell soldier |
| SON | JAMIE, a Campbell soldier |
| DAUGHTER | GLENLYON, a Campbell captain |
| NARRATOR | NARRATOR'S HELPER |

## Costumes

- 3 'uniforms', including Campbell tartan if possible
- plaids or car picnic blankets for father, brother
- nightshirts for grandfather and grandmother
- warm clothing for son and daughter
- shawl for mother
- black clothes for narrator

## Props

- 3 muskets with bayonets
- stone flagon of 'whisky'
- 2 clean white flat double sheets + 2 bloodstained white sheets
- child's doll
- 'baby'
- large cooking pan
- 2 loaves of real bread
- pack of cards
- car rugs for bedding
- bed (as before, p. 116)

## Special Effects

- pre-recorded sounds of screaming, shots, shouts of 'Set it alight', 'Burn them out', 'Don't let him get away' etc., performed by cast
- also two very loud gunshots
- recording of howling, blizzard-type winds
- the 'killings' require choreography to work effectively

## Idea!

Territorial Army cadet corps are a possible source of practice weapons, but please note that even imitation weapons have to be stored securely while on school premises. This play won't work without the use of weapons. If you think they will cause upset, it is best not attempted.

# GLENCOE

*The stage is the interior of a hut, except that stage right is spread with crumpled white sheets, to represent snow.* NARRATOR *sits unobtrusively on edge of stage, hard left. In the bed are* GRANDFATHER *and* GRANDMOTHER. MOTHER *cooks while singing to the baby on her arm. Also present are* FATHER, BROTHER, SON, DAUGHTER. SON *looks out stage left*

SON: Mother! There are soldiers coming! A whole regiment!

FATHER: (*crossing to look for himself*) Campbells. Argyll Highlanders. More than a hundred of them. That's Campbell Glenlyon at their head.

MOTHER: (*grasping* DAUGHTER *by the hand*) Am I to hide the bairns?

FATHER: No . . . no, no . . . We have nothing to fear, do we? The Chief's made his oath of allegiance, hasn't he? England has no quarrel with the MacDonald clan now. No reason to send the Campbells against us, anyway. Let's see why they've come.

(*Enter* GLENLYON)

Do you and your troopers come as friends, Captain?

GLENLYON: As friends. As friends, naturally. My men and I arrived at the garrison at Fort William only to find it was too overcrowded to hold us. So the Master of Stair respectfully asks that the MacDonalds billet us – two or three troopers to a house.

FATHER: For how long?

GLENLYON:  A week – maybe three. We'd pay for our keep
. . . And we'd be greatly obliged to you. Laird MacIain is
agreeable.

FATHER:  (*considers*) Best send two of them in here, then,
out of the cold. Mother, fetch out another loaf. We'll be
breaking bread with the Campbells tonight.

(*Enter two soldiers:* JAMIE *and* ANGUS, *nervously polite.*
MOTHER *fetches a large pan and everyone sits down
round it.*

*Bowls are served and taken to* GRANDPARENTS' *bedside.
The bread is shared out, dipped into the pot, eaten.*
JAMIE *and* FATHER *knock hands in the pot*)

FATHER:  After you.

JAMIE:  No, after you.

GRANDMA: Here's a thing could never have happened in my day. MacDonalds breaking bread with the Campbells – boot-lickers to the English.

BROTHER: Huist, Mammy. The time's gone by for name-calling and blood-letting. Laird MacIain's sworn his allegiance to King William on behalf of the whole MacDonald clan, and there's an end. The Campbells are our allies now – isn't that right, soldier?

JAMIE: (*innocently*) That's right.

ANGUS: (*more knowing*) That's what they tell us . . . Who's for a game of cards?

(FATHER, BROTHER *and* SOLDIERS *play cards while* MOTHER *and* CHILDREN *clear away the meal.* DAUGHTER *shows her doll to* JAMIE *and he shakes hands with it*)

SON: Can I look at your musket, soldier?

JAMIE: Best not. There might be an accident.

(*The action freezes*)

NARRATOR: And so, for fifteen days 120 men of the Earl of Argyll's Highland Regiment stayed in the houses of the MacDonald clan in the great snowy wilderness called Glencoe.

Things were awkward at first. But after a few days, friendships were struck, smiles were smiled, cards were dealt, whisky was drunk, talk flowed more easily.

Then, on the fifteenth evening, Captain Campbell Glenlyon mustered his troops outside the village and issued new orders.

GLENLYON: (*shouts off stage*) Campbells, fall in!

(ANGUS *and* JAMIE *look at each other, jump up and exit smartly stage right.*

BROTHER *goes to look*)

FATHER: What's happening?

BROTHER: I don't know. Glenlyon has them mustered to attention . . . standing easy now. I don't like it. I'm uneasy in my mind. They're checking their muskets. I wish I could hear what Glenlyon is telling them. He's speaking too low.

(*After a time*)

Here they come, back again.

(*Enter* ANGUS *and* JAMIE. JAMIE *is looking shocked, tugging on* ANGUS, *keeping him back from entering the 'hut'*)

JAMIE: But, Angus, it's no' right, I tell you. It's no' honest – or manly!

ANGUS: That's no' for you to say. It's why we're here: to do what we're told.

JAMIE: But we've eaten their bread! We've taken shelter under their roof! It's no' right! It's no' . . . right.

ANGUS: It's orders, that's all. We're soldiers: we follow orders! Good God, Jamie, they're only MacDonalds. Ye've heard what the Master of Stair calls them? Vermin! Ye'd kill vermin, would ye not?

BROTHER: Is something wrong?

ANGUS: No. No. Nothing. Not a thing. Just orders for tomorrow. We have to rise early and go chasing bandits in the glens.

FATHER: In this blizzard?

MOTHER: Best get to your beds, then, I'm thinking, if y'have an early start.

DAUGHTER: Will ye tell me a story, Uncle Jamie?

MOTHER: Leave Jamie be, Jenny: he needs his sleep. And

so do you, my girl.

*(They all climb under blankets.*

*Reasonable wait. Snores from* GRANDFATHER. CHILDREN *turn over in their sleep. Noise of howling wind. More time passes. The* SOLDIERS *sit up, stand up, pick up their muskets and attach bayonets)*

JAMIE: *(still horrified)* Is it five yet? How shall we know when it's five?

*(*ANGUS *puts finger to lips and indicates they should listen for signal)*

ANGUS: Remember: no shooting. Mustn't alert the others. Bayonets only.

*(An owl hoots off stage.* ANGUS *goes to* GRANDFATHER's *bed, wipes his mouth, hesitates, then bayonets* GRANDFATHER)

GRANDMOTHER: Sons! Sons! Get away.

*(She too is killed. The household leaps into life)*

FATHER: *(to* MOTHER) Take the bairns and run! Run, children, run!

*(The* CHILDREN *start to run;* JAMIE *stabs* BROTHER. FATHER *blocks the doorway while* MOTHER *and* CHILDREN *get away down the centre aisle.* MOTHER *is carrying baby and has snatched up a shawl. Exit* SON *and* DAUGHTER. *Noises off of screams, shots. Both* SOLDIERS *point their muskets at* FATHER *who raises arms in surrender)*

FATHER: Let me die in the open air, man, not under my ain roof.

*(*ANGUS *looks uneasily to* JAMIE *for advice)*

Is it so much to ask, from a man whose bread ye've shared?

JAMIE: He's right. It's no' much to ask.

ANGUS: For the bread we've eaten here, ye shall die out of doors.

(*They move out on to the white area. Both* SOLDIERS *raise their muskets to shoot.* FATHER *flings plaid over them and runs. Enter* CAPTAIN GLENLYON)

GLENLYON: (*to Angus*) After him, you fool! He's getting away! . . . And you. (*To Jamie*) There's a woman and bairn run into the forest. Go after them!

(*Exit* GLENLYON *and* ANGUS. NARRATOR *and* HELPER *bring on two sheets, stained with red, and spread them to either side of the stage, covering the dead, cooking pot, bed etc., to look like snowdrifts*)

NARRATOR: More than thirty were killed – nine round one hearth, fourteen locked inside their house and the house set alight. Men, women and children. Everyone under seventy years of age, the order said, and don't trouble the Governor with prisoners.

NARRATOR'S HELPER: Three hundred got away . . . but there was a blizzard blowing. The snow was deep. They were barefoot, in only their nightclothes. They froze to death on the mountainsides. Or they were hunted down.

(MOTHER *stumbles back up aisle to stage, terrified, breathless, followed by* JAMIE. *She climbs back on to the sheeted stage, but falls exhausted. Holds up the baby as* JAMIE *takes aim*)

MOTHER: A curse on all Campbells!

(*Long pause. Off stage: very loud sound of a gun firing twice. It should frighten the audience out of their wits. Pause.* MOTHER *finds herself still alive.*)

Ye fired over my head.

JAMIE: Give me your shawl, woman.

MOTHER: But the cold . . . The baby . . .

JAMIE: I have to have something to show Glenlyon. To prove you're dead.

(*She gives him the shawl and he wipes his bayonet on it*)

Go on. What are you waiting for? Go. Go on. Run!

(*Exit* MOTHER *stage right. Calls after her, but too late for her to hear*)

I'm sorry. I'm so sorry!

(*Exit stage left trailing shawl. Noise of howling wind gets louder and louder, then fades*)

# The Bubble Bursts
## 1720

*Programme note*

In the winter of 1719, gold fever gripped the British public. It had heard that the South Sea Joint Stock Trading Company was set to make millions from South American gold, and that anyone who bought shares could share in those millions . . .

## Cast

| | |
|---|---|
| HICK | BUYERS (as many as desired) |
| JOHNATHAN SWIFT | INK-HOLDER |
| SHARKS | OLD MAN |
| DEALER | QUILL-SELLER |
| 5 PEDLARS | MP, planted in the audience |

## Costumes (*modern dress, with the possible exception of Swift*)

• jewellery, cool-dude clothing, dark glasses for the sharks
• wig and frock coat for Swift if possible
• scruffy clothing for Hick, Quill-seller, Old Man, Ink-holder
• sombrero for donkey-selling Pedlar

## Props (*many optional*)

• *Financial Times*
• broom
• notice and means of fastening it up
• sheaves of paper
• shares tied with ribbon (the more the better)
• a large stone inkwell (or vase)
• 'quill pens'
• bubble wand and liquid
• large copy of *Gulliver's Travels*

## Idea!

Modern get-rich-quick scenes and consumer greed are obvious topics for debate. Some practice is needed in ad-libbing; the buyers must keep up a buzzing frenzy. Pedlars may continue to repeat their lines as they go round the audience, but not so loud as to drown out successive speeches.

# THE BUBBLE BURSTS

DEALER *sits clutching sheaves of paper, but unobtrusively, head lowered.* HICK *stands centre stage leaning on a broom, looking gormless.*

(*Enter* SHARK *holding a Financial Times.*)

SHARK: Tell me, what do you know about stocks and shares, my good man?

HICK: Not a lot. Me mother told me, 'Always share with your friends and keep your legs out of the stocks.'

SHARK: Ah, I don't mean that kind of sharing. I'm talking about your share of good fortune! You have heard of the South Sea Company?

HICK: (*racks his brains*) Nope.

(*Enter* BUYERS *strolling in separately from right and left*)

SHARK: Not heard of the South Sea Company? The fabulously successful joint-stock company that trades with Peru and Chile? You know? (*Loudly, to attract attention*) Where the *gold* comes from?

(*The* BUYERS *converge to listen and become very excited, unlike* HICK)

The South Sea Company sends out galleons laden with nails and cloth and trinkets, and do you know how the natives pay for such cargoes? With bricks of gold, my man! Imagine the profits! Buy a share in the South Sea Company and you can share in those profits. The government has! Why not you?

BUYER 1: I want some of them shares!

BUYER 2: Me too!

BUYER 3: If government has bought shares, it must be safe.

BUYER 4: Yes, where do we go to buy them? How much?

SHARK: You'll have to hurry. Investments like this don't come along every day.

(*The* BUYERS *run off, stage right, with cries of 'let's go', 'what are we waiting for?' The* SHARK *smirks and exits stage left.* HICK *stands where he did, straw in mouth*)

HICK: Me mum told me, 'You never get owt for nowt in this life.'

(*Goes on sweeping the stage and continues to do so for rest of play, sweeping between other characters as they come and go. The* DEALER *at the trestle table sits up abruptly and starts shouting*)

DEALER: Read the prospectus! Fill in the application forms! But don't miss the boat! All aboard for wealth and riches. Take my word for it, folks, the South Sea Company is going to grow very rich indeed, no word of a lie. Share prices are soaring.

(BUYERS *rush on stage eager to buy. They crowd round the table asking for forms, jostling, looking around for a pen to write with, somewhere to fill in their forms. Enter* QUILL-SELLER *and* INK-HOLDER, *bent* OLD MAN *with stick, all shuffling on sideways. Enter* SWIFT *from other side; leans against proscenium nonchalantly, reading Gulliver's Travels*)

SWIFT: (*to audience*) It's true. No word of a lie. The South Sea Company is becoming very rich indeed. Share prices are soaring. But it's not South American gold that's making the directors rich. It's the money of investors like these. Look at them. They can't buy shares fast enough. The talk of gold has turned their heads.

QUILL-SELLER: Quill pens for sale!

INK-HOLDER: Dip your pen in my inkwell! Penny a dip!

OLD MAN: Use my back for a table, sirs. Only a penny for the service.

DEALER: Wait your turn! Wait your turn! I still have a few share certificates left. Just a few.

SWIFT: (*sets down book, produces tub of bubbles and blows some*) My name's Swift. Jonathan Swift, author of novels and pamphlets. I've tried to tell them. It's flim-flam. It's a trick. A bubble.

(*Blows more*)

Attractive. But at heart . . . Nothing. Fresh air.

(*Pops a bubble*)

The man selling the pens – the man lending his bent back

for a table – the ink-holder. Now they are the real businessmen here.

(*Enter the* PEDLARS, *stage right*)

And here come the others. Shrewd shysters who know a good scam when they see one. New joint-stock companies are springing up every day, selling shares in everything from donkeys to dirt.

(*The* PEDLARS *take their trays into the audience and try to sell to audience members*)

PEDLAR 1: (*showing small plank*) Have you heard? There's a new process to make planks from sawdust! Invest! Buy shares! Only the quick will get rich! Shilling a share. Your money will double in a year – honest!

PEDLAR 2: Buy a share in the import of donkeys from Spain. Buy now! Don't wait! Only the quick get rich. Five shillings a share and your money will triple in months! Honest!

(*Enter* SHARKS)

SWIFT: See the basking sharks.

SHARK: I've been in Peru! I've seen gold stacked up in the streets like bricks! Only a fool would pass up a chance to invest in the South Sea...

SWIFT: Bubble.

PEDLAR 3: Have you heard? Perpetual motion has just been perfected! Invest! Only the quick get rich! A guinea a share and your money will quadruple in days! Honest!

PEDLAR 4: (*offers cup of water*) Drink it! Taste it! Only yesterday this was sea water. Invest in a process of turning brine into drinking water. Buy now! Only the quick get rich! Only ten guineas a share.

SHARK: Only a fool would let the opportunity pass!

Invest, invest in the South Sea . . .

SWIFT: Bubble.

PEDLAR 5: Invest in a scheme to refloat the treasure ships of the Spanish Armada! Buy, buy! Only the quick get rich. For only twenty guineas you can be as rich as the King of Spain himself! Honest!

SWIFT: (*saunters across to read a notice being pinned up by* PEDLAR 1) What's this? 'A company for the carrying on of an undertaking of great advantage but nobody to know what it is. Make your fortune overnight.'

(*Looks incredulously at the audience.* BUYERS *crowd round notice.* SWIFT *returns to previous position*)

BUYER 1: I'll buy shares in that!

BUYER 2: So will I!

BUYER 3: (*spiteful*) Ah, but I've just bought the last quill pen!

(QUILL-SELLER *walks off jingling his money. So do* OLD MAN *and* INK-HOLDER. SWIFT *makes clouds of bubbles*)

SWIFT: Suddenly the whole world is full of bubbles.

(*Rising crescendo of cry from everyone as* BUYERS *dash about trying to catch hold of the bubbles*)

ALL: We must buy! Buy! Buy! Buy! Buy! *Buy! Buy!*

(SWIFT *stamps his foot and all but he freeze*)

SWIFT: And then, almost overnight, all the bubbles burst.

(*Watches all the bubbles settle and burst. Only then do* PEDLARS, SHARKS *and* DEALER *make a run for it; exit.*

*The* BUYERS *are left turning and turning around, bewildered. They drop their worthless shares*)

Ordinary people were left without a penny to their name.

(SHARKS *tiptoe furtively across stage: on one side, off the other*)

The directors of the South Sea Company took their money and left the country. Questions were asked in parliament.

(MP *planted in the audience jumps up, points finger and shouts.*

*Meanwhile,* HICK *sweeps the worthless shares over the edge of the stage with his broom*)

MP: How could anyone be so wicked?

How could everyone be so stupid?

Have we become a nation of greedy fools?

SWIFT: But it made no difference. The South Sea Bubble had burst. It almost brought down the government. It almost toppled the King from his throne.

HICK: My mother always said: 'You never get owt for nowt in this life.'

(SWIFT *shakes* HICK *by the hand and they exit, arms round each other's shoulders*)

# 'Give us Back our Eleven Days!'

## 1751

*Programme note*

When, in 1582, Pope Gregory XIII reformed the Julian Calendar, England did not. Two hundred years later, the difference in calendars meant that England and Europe were operating eleven days apart. A well-meaning Earl Chesterfield took it upon himself to put matters right – but never dreamed what a furore he would cause when he turned 3 September into 14 September overnight.

## Cast

| | |
|---|---|
| FATHER | GEORGE |
| MOTHER | ITALIAN PRIEST |
| GRANNY | FRENCH ONION-SELLER |
| SISTER | 6 OTHERS (more if desired) |

## Costumes

- headscarf
- nightdress
- bedroom slippers (modern)
- RC priest's gown
- beret and striped T-shirt
- crowd can be in modern dress
- frock coat and tricorn for Chesterfield

## Props

- placards for mob, reading: GIVE US BACK OUR ELEVEN DAYS; GIVE ME BACK MY BIRTHDAY; I DON'T WANT TO DIE YET; TAXES YES, TIME NO!; IS IT MONDAY OR FRIDAY WEEK?
- ear trumpet
- bed (as before, p. 116)
- shoebrush
- saucepan and rag
- 7 newspapers (for George, and pairs 1, 2 and 4)
- tear-off calendar block
- string of onions

## Special Effects

- recording of grandfather clock ticking and a church clock striking

## Idea!

Try to agree on eleven days which the class could spare out of this year's calendar without anyone losing their birthday.

# 'GIVE US BACK OUR ELEVEN DAYS!'

*The family are in position at the back of the stage,* GRANNY *in the bed on its slope. This time, the bed has for its bedhead a placard, its words not yet showing.* FATHER *is cleaning his boots,* GEORGE *holding an open newspaper,* SISTER *weeping into a handkerchief,* MOTHER *angrily cleaning a pan.*

*(Rest of the characters enter in pairs, one from stage right, one from stage left, walking quickly towards each other, as if on their way somewhere, stopping to speak to their opposite number, as if passing in the street. They meet at different points, not always mid-stage. Having spoken, each continues on his way, but stops just short of leaving the stage)*

FIRST PAIR, A: Have you heard the news?

FIRST PAIR, B: They want us to join Europe!

SECOND PAIR, A: They'll have us talking French next.

SECOND PAIR, B: Or German, or Italian.

ITALIAN PRIEST: (*to* ONION-SELLER) *Benissimo!* Two 'undred yeers ago dey shoulda ha' done it!

FRENCH ONION-SELLER: (*to* PRIEST) *Pourquoi pas? Ce n'est qu'onze jours, quand même!*

THIRD PAIR, A: Chesterfield's got no right! What does he think he's doing?

THIRD PAIR, B: Playing God Almighty. They'll do away with the pound and have us all using the same money soon, you mark my words!

FIRST PAIR:  But we're British!

SECOND PAIR:  We don't want to change.

PRIEST/ONION-SELLER:  You don'a understanda!/*Ils sont fou, les anglais.*

THIRD PAIR:  (*to* PRIEST *and* ONION-SELLER) But how can you have Friday coming after Sunday?

(*Exit all but the family.* GEORGE *reads falteringly from the newspaper . . .*)

GEORGE:  *'Therefore, in order that the Julian Calendar be made to accord with the Gregorian, and England brought into line with Europe, the date of September 3rd shall be changed to September 14th – an adjustment of eleven days.'*

GRANNY:  (*using ear trumpet*) Eh?

FATHER:  That Earl of Chesterfield. Bad enough that he changed New Year from March to January. Since when did a year begin in January, I ask you?

GRANNY:  Eh?

MOTHER:  That's politicians for you. Always wanting to meddle with our lives.

GRANNY:  Eh?

GEORGE:  No, you don't understand. It's just a way of rejigging the calendar.

MOTHER:  Don't interrupt, George.

GEORGE:  It's because a year lasts 365¼ days, and not 365. All those quarters add up after a while . . .

SISTER:  Be quiet, George.

GRANNY:  Eh?

FATHER: They take our money in taxes. Now they even want to take away our days.

MOTHER: Eleven whole days gone from our lives! Think of it.

GEORGE: In Europe they adjusted the calendars years ago, so now there's this gap between England and Europe . . .

ALL: Be quiet, George!

GRANNY: Eh?

MOTHER: (*shouting into the ear trumpet*) They're taking eleven days out of the year, Grandmother.

GRANNY: (*sits up in bed*) They're what?

MOTHER: Eleven days snipped out of September. They mean to miss out Pa's skittles tournament.

SISTER: (*howls*) And my wedding day!

FATHER: Bring rent day eleven days closer, just like that.

GRANNY: (*gets out of bed and puts on headscarf and slippers*) Never mind that! If those rogues take away eleven days, my death will come sooner. And no one's robbing me of eleven days of breathing!

GEORGE: (*calmly soothing*) Oh, Granny, of course you won't die any sooner. It's just a matter of mathematics.

GRANNY: Mathematics be blowed! How you going to go to the Mop Fair, if there isn't a day for the Mop Fair to happen because they've taken away Mop Fair day? Eh? You tell me that!

GEORGE: (*aghast*) No Mop Fair? That's outrageous! They can't do that!

GRANNY: (*purposefully*) Neither shall they, boy. Because we won't let them!

(*Picks up the placard which, up until now, has been her*

*bedhead. The words on the reverse read: 'Give us Back
our Eleven Days')*

People won't stand for it!

    *(Enter* PAIRS 1 AND 2. *They have placards, too)*

FIRST PAIR, A:  We'll put our foot down with a firm hand!

    *(Enter* PAIR 3 *carrying clubs)*

SECOND PAIR, A:  We'll demand they give us back what's
ours!

    *(Enter others carrying placards)*

THIRD PAIR, A:  We'll tell them our lives are short enough
already!

    *(Enter* PRIEST AND ONION-SELLER*)*

ITALIAN PRIEST:  Thissiz getting' outa control!

ONION-SELLER:  *Allons, vite!*

*(They sum up the mood of the growing mob and run off
stage. The action freezes. Enter tricorned gentleman,
haughty, disdainful; stands stage front centre)*

CHESTERFIELD:  *(to audience)* What folly. What muddle-
headedness. Well? Is this the behaviour of intelligent people? The foolish being led astray by the ignorant. Can you
credit it? This . . . mob really believe that a mere alteration
to the calendar will excise eleven days from their miserable little lives. Huh!

GRANNY:  *(to audience)* And how would *you* like it? When
suddenly it's eleven days later than you thought?

THE MOB:  *(chant very softly, then louder)* Give us back
our eleven days!

*(Family incorporate the audience into the chanting in the
following way)*

GEORGE: Who's got a birthday in the next eleven days? Put up your hands! How can you have your birthday on a day that doesn't exist? Well, then, tell them: *Give us back our eleven days!*

SISTER: Who's got an anniversary? No eleven days, no anniversary. Well then, tell them: *Give us back our eleven days!*

MOTHER: Who's got an outing planned? A jolly outing. In the next eleven days? No date, no outing. Well then, tell them: *Give us back our eleven days!*

FATHER: Who's got a pay-day? Eh?

GEORGE: Well, a pocket-money day, then. In the next eleven days. No days, no pocket money! Well then, tell them: *Give us back our eleven days!*

GRANNY: (*using her ear trumpet as a megaphone*) Who's got a lie-in-bed-late-on-Sunday-morning day?

(CHESTERFIELD *puts his hands over his ears, deafened – we hope – by the racket*)

FATHER: Whose mortgage day will come round eleven days sooner?

(*After five or six further repetitions of 'give us back our eleven days', church clock is heard striking loud enough to cut through the noise. Failing that, a loud piano chord silences everyone*)

CHESTERFIELD: Well then . . . well then . . .

(*He looks as if he might relent, then gives a gloating snigger*)

Well then . . . hard luck!

(*Exit to booing. The* MOB *follow in hot pursuit, leaving only the family*)

GRANNY: So now we're eleven days older.

MOTHER: (*to audience*) We threw bricks. We set light to carts. We marched in protest. We shouted ourselves hoarse, but . . . useless.

FATHER: There's no telling these governments anything.

SISTER: We'll get used to it, I suppose.

GRANNY: (*gets wearily back into bed*) We don't have any choice.

GEORGE: But I hope they all remember, when it comes to remarkable dates . . .

SISTER: Saints days.

MOTHER: Christmas.

FATHER: Famous dates.

GRANNY: (*with pause, emphasis*) Millenniums.

GEORGE: It's 'millennia', Granny.

ALL: *Oh, be quiet, George!*

GEORGE: . . . that eleven days were taken out of our calendar. Eleven whole days . . .

(*He holds up a block calendar in his left hand and pulls off eleven sheets one by one, holding on to them all if possible, then scattering them after the last line*)

. . . and thrown away like confetti.

(*Exit all to the loud ticking of clock*)

# Saving Grace
## 1838

## Programme note

When the lighthouse-keeper of the Longstone Lighthouse wrote up his account of the wreck of the *Forfarshire* he wrote simply that nine lives had been 'saved by the Darlings'. This is how those lives were saved.

## Cast

GRACE DARLING
WILLIAM DARLING, her father
BROOKS, her brother
MRS DARLING
SURVIVORS (9 is probably not practical; 5 might be better)

## Costumes

- sou'wester
- hooded cloak for Grace (optional)
- apron for Mrs Darling
- William and Brooks could wear Aran or Breton jumpers to show they are seagoing men

## Props

- mugs
- cards
- stepladder with rope loops for taking oars
- 2 oars (1 each for Grace and William; oars on other side are implied)
- newspaper
- large 'rock' high enough to conceal survivors

## Special Effects

- sound of storm at sea

## Idea!

Discuss lighting. You could consider using an arc lamp to represent the lighthouse lamp. This semi-blinds the audience so that the illusion of darkness and chaos is greater. (Michael Bogdanov was particularly fond of this, at one time.) However, it may just have the undesired effect of making the audience shut their eyes.

# SAVING GRACE

*There is a stepladder to rear of stage with* GRACE *at top.* WILLIAM *foots the ladder.* MRS DARLING *is towards front of stage right, in the 'kitchen'.* BROOKS *is stage left front, narrating. The 'rock' is beyond and behind him, but not so that he masks it. The* SURVIVORS *are, as far as possible, hidden behind the rock. Sea storm sound effects start loud, diminishing*

BROOKS: The sea is hungry tonight, looking for a kill.

MRS DARLING: If only Brooks was home.

BROOKS: Down in the kitchen it's warm and dry.

GRACE: But in the lamp room of the Longstone Lighthouse there is only the lamp's glare and the beam, sharp and cold as steel.

WILLIAM DARLING: The sea hammers on the walls, trying to get inside. It's a bad night for anyone out on a ship.

GRACE: Father! A ship! On Big Harcer! A ship!

*(They change places.* MRS DARLING *freezes, hands against her mouth)*

WILLIAM: Looks like the *Forfarshire*. If it is, there could be upwards of sixty souls aboard. If only Brooks was home.

BROOKS: But I'm not. I'm ashore somewhere warm and dry. Out on Longstone Rock there are only my parents and Grace, my sister.

GRACE: We must do something!

WILLIAM: Nothing we can do. Leastways not till first

light.

BROOKS: So they take it in turns to watch, straining into the dark to see if anyone has pulled themselves out of the crashing sea, out on to Big Harcer Rock. It is a long way to see in the dark, with the rain teeming.

(As GRACE *and* WILLIAM *again change places, the* SURVIVORS *clamber into view*)

SURVIVOR 1: There are some.

SURVIVOR 2: Fewer by the minute.

SURVIVOR 3: Every few waves, the sea carries someone else away or chills the life out of them.

SURVIVOR 4: Waves the size of houses.

SURVIVOR 5: Waves full of timbers and sailcloth.

SURVIVOR 1: And the thunder like cannon-fire.

SURVIVOR 2: Lightning like the devil's trowel prising mussels off a rock.

SURVIVOR 3: Help, somebody! Somebody save us! Help!

(*The other* SURVIVORS *join in calling for help four times*)

MRS DARLING: Those poor souls!

GRACE: It's getting lighter. I can see them now. Men. Women! Children!

WILLIAM: (*putting on sou'wester*) If only Brooks was home.

GRACE: (*descending ladder*) You'll have to make do with me.

BROOKS: Mother knows better than to argue. It is the lighthouse-keeper's duty to do what he can. Besides, how can he stand by and watch the sea take those last nine survivors? And he can't handle the coble on his own, can he?

(GRACE *and* WILLIAM *turn stepladder on its side to be a boat. Increase storm noise so that they have to shout*)

WILLIAM: First the coble has to be launched.

GRACE: Then the oars fitted to the rowlocks.

(*They poke oars through the 'tholepins'*)

The sea pounces at us like a dog, trying to rip us in shreds.

(*More calls for help from* SURVIVORS)

WILLIAM: Hold on! We're coming!

GRACE: (*commentary*) But it's such a long way. (*shouting*) We'll be smashed to pieces if we go nose-on, Father!

WILLIAM: Yeah! We'll have to go in from the side – the lee side.

BROOKS: But that means rowing almost twice as far.

GRACE: I can hardly keep hold of the oars, my hands are so wet and cold!

WILLIAM: (*to* SURVIVORS) Don't give up now! See? Help's coming!

SURVIVOR 1: But it's so far!

SURVIVOR 2: They take so long.

SURVIVOR 3: I can't feel my hands!

WOMAN SURVIVOR: My babies!

SURVIVOR 4: For God's sake, hurry, will you!

GRACE: Every yard we come, we'll have to row back. Already I'm exhausted – frozen. In my woollen underwear, I smell like a drowned sheep.

WILLIAM: Grace! They're too cold to help themselves. You'll have to hold the boat steady while I help them aboard. Can you do it?

GRACE:  Yes, Father! You go! I'll manage.

(GRACE *struggles single-handedly with the 'boat' show-ing it to be almost impossible*)

WILLIAM: (*climbs out and in helping, say, two survivors aboard, says:*) I can only take a few this trip . . .

REMAINING SURVIVORS: (*shout variously*) No!/Don't go without us!/Wait!/Don't leave us!/For pity's sake!

WILLIAM:  We'll come back for you! Hold on! We'll come back!

(*They row back. As boat is unloaded into the 'kitchen'*
MRS DARLING *gives out mugs of tea and mimed blan-kets, indicates warmth of stove with outstretched hands.*
*Improvised comments. By mime,* WILLIAM *asks for help with the second voyage. One of the* SURVIVORS *volunteers*)

BROOKS: Three trips the coble made between the light-house and Big Harcer, there and back. There and back.

MRS DARLING: Our little kitchen filled up with frozen, wretched people, but he kept going out again, my William. Out into the storm.

(WILLIAM *and* VOLUNTEER *repeat the journey just once then he and* GRACE *struggle to stand ladder up again as if securing the boat.* WILLIAM *falls to his knees with weariness. Meanwhile, the* SURVIVORS (*except* WOMAN) *describe in mime to* MRS DARLING *how* GRACE *rowed, held boat still etc., and interject:*)

SURVIVOR 1: Marvellous girl!

SURVIVOR 2: Wait till people hear.

SURVIVOR 3: Deserves a medal, she does.

SURVIVOR 4: Deserves a reward.

WOMAN SURVIVOR: My babies!

BROOKS: If only I'd been there.

GRACE: (*confused by the praise*) What else could I do?

(*Exit* SURVIVORS, *still saying thank you, stage right.* BROOKS *crosses stage and hands the family an open newspaper which they read*)

BROOKS: I'm not jealous. Don't get me wrong. I didn't envy our Grace the fame in the papers, or that medal or that reward she was given.

WILLIAM: No. It was the neighbours who marred it all.

MRS DARLING: You would have thought she had wrecked the ship herself, to hear some of them.

GRACE: There was hate mail – poison-pen letters.

MRS DARLING: Take no notice, my love. We know how it really was.

BROOKS: The sea feels cheated, too. Listen to it. Hammering on the walls. Trying to get in. Trying to get its own back.

GRACE: It does get in, too. Its sodden, salty breath comes in between the bricks. Sometimes I feel like the lighthouse, surrounded by wetness. It hammers up against me. Forces its way inside me.

(*Coughs. Then brightens up and beams*)

Queen Victoria herself wrote me a letter! Imagine! A letter from the Queen!

(*She leaves unobtrusively*)

BROOKS: (*proud and affectionate*) And all over the country, our Gracie is famous. People hang pictures of her and Dad on their walls.

WILLIAM: Fancy. Me and Gracie on people's walls.

MRS DARLING: Cards, anyone?

BROOKS: If only Gracie was here.

WILLIAM: (*concentrating on cards*) Not for us to question the ways of the Almighty. Fame is no cure for consumption.

BROOKS: I know. All the same . . .

BROOKS/MRS DARLING/WILLIAM: If only Gracie was still here.

(*They continue to play cards, then one by one say 'I'm out', lay down cards and exit till stage is empty. Sea storm noise returns, very loud*)

# Father of Nobody's Children
## 1869

*Programme note*

Thomas Barnardo was planning a missionary career in China. He had already given up studies in medicine and was teaching poor children in London's East End while he waited for the chance to go. Then one evening, ten-year-old Jim Jarvis seemed unwilling to go home . . .

## Cast

THOMAS BARNARDO

JIM JARVIS

8 STREET 'BOYS' INCLUDING 1 GIRL

## Costumes

- cap for Jim
- no shoes for the boys/girls
- clothes as ragged as possible, some children in vests; lots of dirt
- Barnardo was twenty-one, wore blue-tinted wire-framed glasses, and was hardly taller than a child himself

## Props

- stepladder
- several large cardboard boxes, with graffiti
- blackboard, already chalked up
- books and exercise books
- teacher's table
- old-fashioned lift-lid school desk
- 2 wooden chairs
- 2 plates of 'food'
- 2 knives and forks
- tablecloth
- gin bottles
- axe, boot, clothes brush, modern courier's pannier
- milk bottle

## Special Effects

- if lighting is available, stage left can be illuminated and stage right left dark until Barnardo reaches the top of the ladder
- the stepladder must have non-slip feet and stabilisers
- pre-recording of school bell followed by children rushing out of school

## Idea!

Have children write to Shelter to find out the number of people estimated to be sleeping rough each night. Write to Barnardo's to see how their work has changed in recent times. Both charities have e-mail addresses:

*info@shelter.org.uk*
*webmaster_barnardos@compuserve.com*

# FATHER OF NOBODY'S CHILDREN

*A stepladder centre stage and side-on to the audience supports a blackboard. On the side visible is written: 'Go ye into all the world and preach the gospel.' On the other, 'Dr Barnardo's home for boys'. Stage left is brightly lit. Stage right is left as dark as possible and strewn with three or four cardboard boxes facing the audience and daubed with Victorian graffiti. E.g. PEELERS WILL SKIN YOU. JACK THE RIPPER IS INNOCENT. SIGN THE CHARTER! FREE GIN FOR MOTHERS etc. The* STREET BOYS *lie curled up and keeping very still so as not to catch the eye*

(*The pre-recorded noise of children leaving school.* BARNARDO *and* JIM *hold still until the noise fades to silence.* BARNARDO *stands at his desk putting his things away.* JIM *fiddles around by his desk*)

BARNARDO: Home-time, Jim. Hurry along now.

(JIM *continues to fiddle about*)

Jim? I said hurry along. Your mother will be expecting you.

JIM: Ain't got no mother, sir.

BARNARDO: I'm sorry. Your father, then.

JIM: Ain't got one of them, neever. Never had one of them. S'fearful cold out. Couldn't I sleep here tonight, sir? Just kip down by the stove? Wouldn't steal nuffink.

BARNARDO: Don't be absurd, Jim! I'm going home to my supper and you're going home to yours. Run along, there's a good boy.

(JIM *goes to leave, unwillingly*)

Where is it you live, then Jim?

JIM: Oo, here 'n there. Around and about. There was some haycarts up Covent Garden yesterday, but they's gone today.

BARNARDO: (*to audience*) I didn't believe him. I didn't want to. Would you? I'd heard tell of children living on the streets, but I thought the phrase was . . . well, melodramatic. An exaggeration. Oh, I knew all about poverty; I was teaching in a Ragged School, after all. But children living on the streets? Hardly.

JIM: Couldn't I sleep here tonight, sir? Cosy in here, what wiv the stove.

BARNARDO: (*to audience*) I wanted to get home. I was tired. I'd been teaching for ten hours. And teaching was only a temporary job for me. I was just killing time. Waiting to go to China, to tell the poor heathens about Jesus. (To JIM) I told you, Jim. No.

(JIM *goes to leave, as before*)

But you may come for a bite of supper at my house, if you care to.

JIM: Yes please, sir!

(BARNARDO *gets out two plates from inside his desk. They take down the blackboard and set it on top of the desk, put on a tablecloth and move their chairs. They are at* BARNARDO's *house, eating*)

JIM: (*talking with full mouth*) Sometimes the peelers come and move us on. Sometimes the rats get too bad, so we have to give ground, sort of thing.

BARNARDO: (*to audience*) I didn't want to believe him.

JIM: Had a job once, on the canals, but every time the bargee drank he knocked seven bells out of me. So I run off. Someone says: go up the Ragged School, they got a stove there. You can maybe sleep in there.

BARNARDO: Jim, tell me, are there other boys who do what you do? Sleep where they can, I mean? Out in the open?

JIM: (*laughs loudly*) You joking, sir? 'Course there is! Any number! Show you, if you want. Shall I? Want to see?

BARNARDO: (*to audience*) No. I wanted my bed. I wanted to go to China. I wanted to convert the heathen. I wanted Jim Jarvis not to exist. (To JIM) Yes. Yes, Jim. Show me.

(BARNARDO *takes off the tablecloth, and* JIM *wears it round him like a shawl. They weave a complex course around the set*)

Where are you taking me? It's past midnight, you know.

JIM: Not far, sir. Don't never have to go far to find my kind. If you know where to look.

(*They reach the stepladder and* JIM *points up it*)

Plenty up there, always.

BARNARDO: On the roof?!

JIM: On the roofs. Down the sewers. In the carts. Down the docks.

(BARNARDO *climbs the stepladder slowly and unwillingly, looking round at* JIM *who foots the ladder.*

*He peers down from the top. Increased lighting reveals children curled up inside and outside the cardboard boxes. They stir in their sleep, one by one*)

BARNARDO: (*to audience*) There were so many of them! Ragged and half-starved and frozen.

JIM: Want me to wake 'em, sir? I'll wake 'em up if you like!

BARNARDO: *No!* (To audience) Then they would look at me with those hollow eyes. They would clamour at me for food. Besides, it was kinder to let them sleep. Cruel to wake them.

(*The whole stage springs into action, the sleeping* BOYS *jumping up and fetching the blackboard back to the stepladder, this time displaying the other side; they put down a doormat and milk bottle to represent a front door.* BOYS 5, 6, 7 *fetch axe, boot and brush out of* JIM's *desk*)

BOY 1: It was like a dream come true.

BOY 2: He opened this home for homeless boys.

GIRL: And another one for girls.

BOY 3: He turned drinking dens into tea-halls.

BOY 4: He turned drunkards into preachers.

JIM: He gave hundreds of talks, telling folks about the night he met me. Called hisself *Dr* Barnardo. Weren't no doctor really, but who cares? Could've called hisself the King of Siam for all I minded.

BARNARDO: I suddenly realised: God didn't want me to go to China at all! He wanted me here, in England, putting some hope back into the lives of these loveless, homeless children!

BOY 5: (*with axe*) Trained us to be wood-choppers.

BOY 6: (*with despatch-rider's pannier*) City messengers.

BOY 7: (*with boot*) Boot-makers.

BOY 1: (*with brush*) Brush-makers.

BOY 2: Found us families who wanted us.

BOY 3: Gave us love till someone else would.

BOY 4: He never turned no one away.

BOY 8: Except me.

(*Action freezes, except for* BOY 8 *who knocks at the 'door'.* BARNARDO *opens*)

BARNARDO: There's no room. I'm sorry. We are completely full up. Come back tomorrow.

BOY 8: (*doing as he describes*) I had nowhere else to go. There was nowhere else to go. So I just curled up there on the doorstep, waiting for morning. So cold. So frightened. So hungry . . .

BOY 5: (*opens door to put out a milk bottle*) Sir! Doctor Barnardo, sir! Come quick.

(BARNARDO *comes. Checks the body*)

He's dead, sir.

BARNARDO: I swore then that no child would ever again be turned away or refused help.

BOY 6: Soon there were Barnardo Homes all over.

BOY 7: Sixty thousand kids taken in, just in his lifetime.

JIM: Not that it's the same these days.

BOY 1: Yeah. Those were the Victorian times.

BOY 2: No one living on the streets nowadays.

BOY 3: No one homeless. No one unloved.

BOY 8: No one sleeping cold and hungry in a doorway.

(*The school bell rings, as before, and the* BOYS *jump about and race off stage, shouting and yelling and laughing, followed by* BARNARDO *who glances round the empty stage without seeing* BOY 8 *still curled up stage front centre*)

# Votes for Women!

## 1913

## *Programme note*

Emily Davison had been to gaol many times before, for demonstrating in favour of votes for women. On Derby Day, June 1913, she decided to make one more protest which could not fail to attract public attention.

## Cast

| | |
|---|---|
| BOOKIE | PUNTER I |
| SUFFRAGETTE | WOMAN PUNTER |
| EMILY DAVISON | JOLLY WOMAN |
| TICKET SELLER | SOUR PUNTER |
| TIPSTER | OLD PUNTER |
| COMMENTATOR | TWO POLICEMEN |

## Costumes

- Emily in white gloves, long coat worn over short flapper dress
- railway cap
- straw hats for all women
- trilbies for bookie and commentator
- police helmets

## Props

- handbag
- wooden box to stand on
- binoculars
- protester's placard: VOTES FOR WOMEN
- soft bread roll to throw

## Special Effects

- sound of galloping racehorses

## Idea!

Discuss what kind of protests political agitators have employed – from letter bombs to hunger strikes. Which are 'acceptable' to the group? Which have proved the most successful historically?

# VOTES FOR WOMEN!

BOOKIE *stands on box, stage right, shouting the odds as more and more people drift on to the stage; all except* EMILY *and railway* TICKET SELLER

BOOKIE: Place your bets, gentlemen! Place your bets! 5 to 4 on a Balkan massacre; 8 to 1 on Prohibition ending; opening bets on Panama Canal; 10 to 1 bar.

(*Enter* SUFFRAGETTE *protester with placard: VOTES FOR WOMEN*)

PUNTER 1: (*snide*) What odds will you give us on Votes for Women?

(*General laughter and hilarity*)

BOOKIE: Don't make me laugh. There's a non-starter if ever there was one!

TIPSTER: Suffragettes? They can burn all the letter-boxes in Piccadilly and chain themselves to every railing in town – they'll still be a bunch of old no-hope nags.

WOMAN PUNTER: Slashing pictures and smashing windows! Hooligans, that's all they are.

(*She shies a missile at the* SUFFRAGETTE's *placard*)

OLD PUNTER: Ought to be home in their kitchens, cooking dinner for their menfolk!

JOLLY WOMAN: Ought to know their place.

SOUR PUNTER: Ought to be locked up.

(POLICE *rush on and arrest* SUFFRAGETTE *while* PUNTERS *cheer. Into space vacated by protester comes a railway* TICKET SELLER, *then* EMILY DAVISON *dressed in*

*long coat, white gloves and with handbag.* PUNTERS *etc.*
*form an impatient queue behind her*)

EMILY:  One ticket to Epsom Downs, please.

TICKET SELLER:  Yes, miss. Return or single?

EMILY:  Oh! Er . . . I never thought . . . I, er . . .

TICKER SELLER:  Well? Are you coming back, or not? Must know, surely! Be quick! Train can't wait while you make up your mind, you know.

EMILY:  Return. Thank you.

TICKET SELLER:  Going to the Derby, then?

EMILY:  (*startled*) Yes. Yes, I am.

TICKET SELLER:  You and the rest of the world. Have fun.

(*The queue breaks away and begins dancing and*
*chanting, arm in arm.*


EMILY *shrinks away from them, demure and nervy*)

ALL BUT EMILY:  Going to the Derby, looking very smart,
  Going to the Derby in my little donkey cart
  Passing all the crackpots, just like a tart,
  Going to the Derby in my little donkey cart!

(*Repeat*)

JOLLY WOMAN:  (*breaking away from dancers to befriend*
EMILY. *The* DANCERS *repeat the song once more, softly*)
Lovely outing, in't it? Derby Day. Only time my Les and I have a flutter. Don't hurt, do it? Not just once a year!

EMILY:  I . . . er . . .

TIPSTER:  Want a sure thing, miss? I can tell you a sure thing! Flannery's Pony! A Derby-winner if ever a horse stood on four legs!

EMILY: I . . . er . . .

JOLLY WOMAN: Nah! We'll bet on the King's 'orse, won't we, luv? Ain't patriotic hardly to bet on anyfing but the King's 'orse. Not in the Derby. Derby's special. In't that right, luv?

TIPSTER: Be lucky if you get 5 to 4 on Anmer. Everyone always goes for the King's 'orse. Never make a killing that way.

EMILY: (*panicky*) Make a killing?

TIPSTER: Yeah! You need an outsider to make a killing! A nice 100 to 1 outsider.

(*Meanwhile, the crowd all lunge cheerfully to one side of the stage leaving* EMILY *isolated stage left*)

EMILY: An outsider. Yes.

(BOOKIE *gets on to box again. People wag money at him*)

BOOKIE: All right! All right! Here are the odds I'm offering: 5 to 4 on Anmer! War of the Sexes 16 to 1. Man's Tops, 7 to 10 on. Free and Equal isn't a runner! Rhyme and Reason scratched.

COMMENTATOR: The runners are circling in the enclosure now! Look them over and place your bets! Good afternoon, ladies and gentlemen. Welcome to the 1913 Derby!

(*The actors* (*except for* EMILY *and* JOLLY WOMAN) *circle the stage as if they themselves have become the horses*)

EMILY: Which is the King's horse?

JOLLY WOMAN: That one there! The bay. Anmer. Don't know nothing about the races, me, but I can tell the King's 'orse. The Derby's different, innit? The Derby's special. Everyone takes notice of the Derby.

EMILY: (*to audience, sombrely*) The Derby's special.

Everyone takes notice of the Derby.

(COMMENTATOR *faces front but the rest stop being
horses and form into a dense block of spectators at front
of stage looking upstage*)

COMMENTATOR: And they're off! The 1913 Derby is
under way! It's Man's Tops in the lead with Laissez Faire
pressing hard. There's Pretty Lady on the rails . . . Looks
as if Pankhurst's boxed in!

THE CROWD: (*start to shout encouragements like:*) Come
on, Anmer!/Move yourself!/Use the whip, you
fool!/Anmer's moving up!/What's the matter with you?
etc.

EMILY: (*faces audience, wipes her mouth with a handkerchief then puts handkerchief into handbag and puts bag
down on ground. Turns round and starts to watch as
intently as the rest. After a moment says quietly:*) Votes
for Women!

(*Then louder*)

Votes for Women!

(*She worms her way through the crowd and out of sight,
shouting loudly:*)

Votes for Women!!

(*Horse neighs. Loud stamp from crowd who then gasp.
Each turns round in speaking, as if revolted by what
they have seen*)

PUNTER 1: Oh my God.

TIPSTER: Someone on the ground.

SOUR PUNTER: It's Anmer! The King's horse is down!

JOLLY WOMAN: She tried to snatch the reins.

BOOKIE: But the horse ran into her – fell over her.

WOMAN PUNTER: Kicking its legs. Foam on its mouth. Poor beast. Is it hurt?

JOLLY WOMAN:  And that girl underneath.

COMMENTATOR:  A suicide, was it?

BOOKIE:  She threw herself under its hooves. I'd give odds on it.

JOLLY WOMAN:  Probably been jilted by some lad.

TICKET SELLER:  No, no! She tried to snatch the reins. She shouted something. Didn't you hear?

PUNTER 1:  She's a suffragette, that's what.

*('Men' and 'women' separate to either side of the stage)*

WOMAN PUNTER:  'Votes for Women,' she said.

BOOKIE:  A publicity stunt, was it? Gone wrong?

JOLLY WOMAN:  A grand gesture.

SOUR PUNTER:  Hysterical female. Typical!

JOLLY WOMAN:  The ultimate sacrifice.

COMMENTATOR:  Ruined Derby Day for all these people. Right selfish, I call it.

JOLLY WOMAN:  Gave her life to further her cause . . .

WOMAN PUNTER:  Is the horse all right?

(*Crowd mingles again*)

TICKET SELLER:  (*picks up handbag and looks inside*) Her name's Emily Davison. No betting slips. (*To audience*) A return ticket, look. What does that mean, do you suppose? A spur of the moment thing?

BOOKIE:  A publicity stunt gone wrong. I'd lay odds.

JOLLY WOMAN:  Too late to ask now. Emily Davison is dying.

(*Exit all sadly or resentfully (except for* BOOKIE *and* COMMENTATOR) *in a tight huddle so that Emily too can get off stage*)

COMMENTATOR:  (*looks out into the audience with binoculars as he says:*) They're lining up now for the next race. And they're off! And it's the Great War coming up. Suffragette has given way to Patriotic Woman. The going's heavy, but Patriotic Woman is holding up. So-Many-Men . . . So-Many-Men down! Yes! So-Many-Men brought down by the Great War. That's going to change the odds. No sign of Votes for Women yet, but who knows? In this kind of race, anything is possible.

(*Freezes. Enter* EMILY *dressed as flapper. Pause. Silence. She and the* BOOKIE *eye each other across the stage*)

BOOKIE: What, you again?

EMILY: What odds are you offering now on Votes for Women?

BOOKIE: All bets are off. No odds. What d'you think I am? Made of money? This is 1925, miss. We ain't livin' in the Dark Ages here. Votes for Women is a racing certainty.

(*Exit* EMILY, *dancing and laughing*)

More's the pity. (*To commentator*) They'll be running for parliament next.

COMMENTATOR: Never!

(*Reflecting on this they exit, shaking their heads and both agreeing:*)

Nah. Never!

# No-Man's Land

## 1914

*Programme note*

Nine million died in the Great War of 1914–18.
Several who survived (and others who did not)
testified to one extraordinary Christmas when
peace broke out amid the barbed wire of no-
man's land.

## Cast

CIGS
PEN
4 or 5 other BRITISH SOLDIERS
5–6 GERMAN SOLDIERS

## Costumes

- ideally everyone in long, shapeless 'greatcoats'
- British and German helmets
- faces and hands should be dirty

## Props

- rifles
- 2 white handkerchiefs
- bottle
- brown leather football
- 2 packs of cigarettes (mime roll-your-owns)
- notepaper and pencil × 2
- Union Jack and Prussian flag

## Special Effects

- sound effects of heavy gunfire, machine-guns, shells exploding
- optional music for scene setting: e.g. 'There's a long, long trail a-winding'
- 'scenery' can consist of a token coil of barbed wire (without the barbs of course) snagged with pieces of red and khaki rag
- the footballing has to be very carefully controlled so that the ball does not escape into the audience. The fraternising must not be rushed; it is the core of the play

## Idea!

This is an ideal play for Poppy Day and the pre-Christmas term. Print the words of the final hymn in your programme, so that the audience can join in.

# NO-MAN'S LAND

*On either side of the stage the* GERMANS *and* BRITISH *huddle in their 'trenches', hidden from one another by two lines of cartons or tea chests, leaving the centre stage or 'no-man's land' empty but for poppies strewn about. The actors' positions should exactly mirror each other: one yawns, his counterpart yawns; one sneezes, his counterpart sneezes; one rocks in terror, one cleans his gun, one writes a letter, so do their counterparts*

(CIGS (*and counterpart) roll a cigarette. Noise stops. A bird starts singing*)

CIGS: You still writing home? What do you find to say? About the mud? The stench? The rats? How many died yesterday? The wounded out in no-man's land screaming all night?

PEN: (*not in response to* CIGS, *but as if we are hearing his thoughts*) 'Dear Ma, Just a line to say I am well and chipper. There was a special issue of apple jam this morning – very tasty. We had plum last week, but it wasn't like yours. Very bitter.'

CIGS: Do you tell 'em about going over the top, knowing there's a machine-gun waiting? If he don't get you, you can drown in a foxhole or go blind in the gas, if you don't get hung up on the wire. Do you let on we only go over 'cos the officers shoot us if we don't?

PEN: 'More gloves would be handy. Socks too, if you can spare the time. I was glad to hear about Daisy's birthday party. I'd rather be spending Christmas at home with you all, but can't be helped, eh? When King and country calls . . .'

CIGS: Christmas? Reckon they don't hold Christmas here in hell.

GERMAN 1: (*starts singing*) *Stille Nacht, heilige Nacht*
*Alles schlaft, einsam wacht*
*nur das traute hoch heilige Paar.*
*Holder Knabe im lokkigen Haar,*
*schlaf in himmlischer Ruh,*
*schlaf in himmlischer Ruh!*

PEN: (*partway through verse*) Listen!

CIGS: Must be the Welsh Fusiliers. They can't help themselves.

PEN: No. No. It's Gerry. It's the Bosch.

(*All* GERMANS *join in, repeating first verse. The* BRITISH *gradually join in, too, singing the English words*)

Silent Night, Holy Night,
All is calm, all is bright,
Round yon Virgin mother and child,
holy Infant so tender and mild,
Sleep in heavenly peace!
Sleep in heavenly peace.

(*A football is thrown from the wings, or front row of audience, into centre stage. Everyone crouches, takes cover, arms over their heads. Little by little they emerge, still mirroring each other's movements.* PEN *peers over barricade*)

PEN: It's a football.

CIGS: Don't be daft. Who'd bring a football to France with them?

PEN: It is, though. It's a football.

(GERMAN *with gun raises white handkerchief on tip of rifle*)

Gerry wants a truce!

*(He gets out his own handkerchief and waves it)*

CIGS:  *(tries to restrain* PEN*)* You're never going out there? What about the snipers? It's a trick.

PEN:  No. No. It isn't.

*(*GERMAN 1 *climbs out.* PEN *climbs out. In pairs they repeat this until everyone is standing about awkwardly in no-man's land. One tentatively kicks the ball. A game begins. Laughter develops. Finally* BRITISH *kick ball off-stage to shouts of 'goal!' and 'torpfosten!' The men exchange cigarettes without speaking. A bottle passes round. They show each other photographs of loved ones. They compare uniforms/wounds. Noise of a shell whining overhead sends them all scurrying back to their trenches. Two are left facing each other, however:* CIGS *and* GERMAN 2*)*

CIGS:  Happy Christmas, Gerry.

GERMAN 2:  Huh?

PEN: (*calls translation*) Alles Gute zum Weihnachten.

GERMAN I: (*pops up from his trench again*) Ah! Ja! Alles
Gute zum Neujahr, Tommy.

(*They adopt identical positions once more. The noise of
gunfire builds up. PEN screws up the letter he was writing and begins again*)

PEN: 'Dear Ma, Something wonderful happened here
today. Can't say much. Censor wouldn't let me. Tell you
about it when I get home. But we had a kind of Christmas
here today. Honest. A Christmas like none I ever saw. Like
no one ever saw. Not in two thousand years of
Christmases.'

CIGS: Christmas! In hell, eh?

PEN: (*still writing*) So Peace on Earth. Goodwill. All that.
Just for a while: peace. Puts me in mind of that other
song. How did it go?

(*Sucks his pen and thinks. Begins by trying to remember
the words of a hymn, then begins singing it to himself.
Line by line the others join in. It is hoped the audience
will as well*)

For now the time is something, something . . .

(*sings tentatively*)

By prophet bards foretold,
When with the ever-circling years
Comes round the Age of Gold,
When peace shall over all the earth
Its ancient splendours fling,
And the whole world give back the song
Which now the angels sing!

(*Before the song finishes, the actors begin to place their
rifles star-form in no-man's land and pick up a poppy
instead, then to exit so that ultimately the stage is left
empty*)

# Jolly Jack

*Extra Material to Unify an Assortment of Plays Acted by the Same Team of Actors*

# JOLLY JACK

*The actors start off as a troop of mummers, entering up aisle, and pushing the props basket along in a wheelbarrow. They are dressed in simple black, wearing one of the hats they will wear during the coming plays. They are led by* JOLLY JACK *who is playmaster. (This character can take charge of scene/costume changes between each play, ordering the actors around as if they are under his direction)*

JOLLY JACK: In comes I, Jolly Jack, wife and family at my back.
In comes us, actors all
Tales to tell, within this hall
Stories from three* thousand years
Of blood and sweat and toil and tears.

(* or two or one, as appropriate)

INDIVIDUALS: (*in turn, forming a circle onstage*) Rich man . . .
   Poor man . . .
      Beggarman . . .
         Thief

JOLLY JACK: Root and trunk and branch and leaf.

Hand and heart and tongue and eye.

INDIVIDUALS: (*in turn*) Tinker . . .
   Tailor . . .
      Soldier . . .
         Spy . . .

JOLLY JACK: (*indicating the costumes and set*) These our tatters, these our lands.

All our fame is in your hands.
In comes us, actors all
For to tell, within this hall,
Of farce . . . and scam . . . and mystery
Wars . . . adventures . . . victory

ALL: Stories from *your* history!

# Interval

JOLLY JACK: Tom and Harry and Dick and Jack

Are going now, but we'll be back;

For that old saying holds good still:

Every Jack must have his gill.

ALL THE REST: (*Protest and hold up finger and thumb to show smallness of one gill*) One gill?

    (*General mutterings about how thirsty they are*)

JOLLY JACK: Well maybe a pint or two, then. Who's buying?

REST: (*variously*) Not me!/You are!/They are!

    (*Exit all, with property basket between them*)

# Entrance, second half

(*All reel in drunkenly, leaning on each other, bringing replenished property basket*)

JOLLY JACK: In comes us, your troubadours,

To dance and laugh and weep and roar.

ONE OBSERVER: Hey! Hang on. Maybe they're not enjoying themselves. Maybe they'd rather go home now!

(*They all peer out into the audience*)

JOLLY JACK: That's very true – so – what do you say? (*Asks audience*) Shall we carry on with another play?

(*Roars of encouragement from the audience (we hope)*)

Okay!

# Epilogue

(*As the props basket is carried out through the audience, by the cast,* JOLLY JACK *is last to leave*)

JOLLY JACK: One more day has just become
A piece of history: over, done.
So out goes I, Jolly Jack,
Wife and family at my back.
Out go we, your troubadours.
Tides wash clean Britannia's shores;
Let them wash away our flaws.
The rest is silence . . . or applause.

(*Runs gleefully out*)